Start Your Own Amazon Store
...without getting hurt

Lori Dunham

Copyright © 2017 Dunham Global Ventures, Inc.

All Rights Reserved. No part of this book may be reproduced or transmitted in any form or by any means, electronic or mechanical, including photocopying, recording, or by any information storage and retrieval system, without permission in writing.

Printed in the United States of America

ISBN-13: 978-1985413160

ISBN-10: 1985413167

Disclaimers:

The use of the name "Amazon" is for reference purposes only, referring only to their publicly-released information, website features, tool and resources available to those affiliates who want or have an "Amazon Store" hosted by Amazon.com, Amazon.mx, Amazon.ca or any entity associated with Amazon, Inc. No information in this book binds Amazon to perform, in any capacity, outside of its published Terms of Use provided on their public website.

Trademarked names that appear in this work are used for editorial purposes only, with no intention of infringement of the respective owner's trademark.

This work is not intended to be the only answer to finding success on Amazon, but rather, a suggested path. As with any business venture, it is the reader's responsibility to conduct full due diligence regarding the safe and successful operation of a business. Full and complete risk associated to investment and money is assumed to be at the reader's discretion and expense. There are many variables to consider when reaching for success. Business methodology and acumen is important to finding success; however, desired results could also be linked to marketplace demand, product supply, individual drive and experience, as well as, reliance on tools, websites and resources not under direct control. There is no guarantee, expressed, or implied, that using the information in this work will produce the same results as the author, improve personal financial standings or make any money. The information shared in this work is for the reader's own personal use only.

By reading this work, taking any action based on the information provided, or taking no action at all, the reader assumes all associated risks, and fully acknowledges that the reader, solely, is responsible for any outcome, regardless of how the information shared in this work was interpreted. The author cannot be held responsible in any way for the success or failure of a business, in any manner, as a result of the information shared in this work.

In accordance with the Federal Trade Commission's policy to be forthcoming about any affiliate relationships presented in this work, if an affiliate relationship exists, it will be specifically noted. Following the links within this work, or on the author's website, and, subsequently visiting affiliate sites, may create a cookie in the web browser, and upon further purchases, the author could receive additional compensation.

No part of this work may be resold, reprinted, reproduced, transmitted, or distributed in any form or by any means, electrical or mechanical, including photocopying and recording, or by any information storage or retrieval system without permission in writing from Dunham Global Ventures, Inc. It is strictly prohibited to reproduce the content enclosed herein or to distribute this work to any third party, or via any third-party website. All content in this guide is protected by legal copyright ©.

The information contained in this work is provided 'as is' without warranty of any kind. The entire risk as to the results and the performance of the information is assumed by the user or reader, and in no event shall Lori Dunham, Dunham Global Ventures, Inc., or any associated affiliate be liable for any consequential, incidental, or direct damages suffered in the course of using the information in this work.

Dedication

For
Catherine

Acknowledgements

To Carey:
Thank you for believing in me and taking on the risk to start this amazing journey. Everyone needs hope, and you gave that spark back to me.

To Maddy:
You are a sincere and faithful friend, always praying for me, and reminding me of how much God loves me and wants to delight in the prosperity of His children. Thank you for standing in the gap for me as I figure out my journey – this is only just the beginning.

To Brian, my brother:
Thank you for giving me a chance to reconcile and become a part of your life – again. It is indeed a great blessing to know you and experience the wonderful man you have become.

To the AMAZING coaches and mentors at Live Out Loud, Inc.:
My deepest gratitude for your willingness to support my dreams, to encourage me to act and to cheer me on through the wildest ride I have ever experienced. I am so honored to be a part of the family. Thank you for welcoming me.

Finally, there are many whom cannot be named who helped me in ways too numerous to express here. Through their words or actions, they have guided my path toward this book. THANK YOU!

Contents

I.	Foreword	1
II.	Introduction	5
III.	First Things First	10
IV.	Getting Started	14
V.	Decide How to Sell	32
VI.	Choosing products	39
VII.	Where to get products	55
VIII.	Building Listings and Preparing Products for Sale	65
IX.	Tracking a Shipment	111
X.	Customer Interaction	113
XI.	Payments and Deposits	123
XII.	Legal, Taxes and Reports in Amazon	125
XIII.	Support and Troubleshooting	126
XIV.	Conclusion: Now what?	128
XV.	Directory of Resources	130
XVI.	Testimonials	131

I.

Foreword

When Lori asked me to write the foreword for her book, I immediately agreed. Why? Because I knew it was written with moral, ethical, and positive intentions. Her book is a labor of love that has taken her a lot of heartache and headache to produce. As a marketer and speaker, I know the world is changing and we need more individuals like Lori making a positive change in the world. I met Lori when I gave a speech about empowering women through entrepreneurship and she immediately touched me as someone who had not only embraced the message, but was going to take it upon herself to do her part. I was pleasantly surprised to see her become an author and public speaker herself.

Like many others, Lori knew she had a book within but never thought someone would be interested in her message. She of course was wrong, as we all have something to contribute, sometimes we just cannot see that in ourselves. After I met her in June 2017, she immediately took action, by August she had found the encouragement and by October her book was in pre-sale.

Lori is a testimony that where there is a will, there is a way. She wrote her book based on her own personal experiences, and struggles she faced after coming home tired from a full-time job. In this book, she shares the techniques she has learned and personally utilized in establishing her own online business, achieving financial independence on her terms, without compromise. My goal when I embarked on my speaking career was to empower and enlighten individuals to step out of their comfort zone and strive to be the person they dreamed of becoming when they were children; achieving their dreams. Lori is a perfect example of what modern women can do, what we can all do if we believe and focus. The miracle of belief has opened her up to a positive mindset that has generated a positive result. She helps individuals establish their own online business. Her system is not an overnight fix, it is a systematized model of how she went from being paralyzed emotionally to regaining her self-esteem and attaining the level of success she always dreamed of. She utilized unconventional education to break the barriers she saw before her, sometimes frightening, horrifying situations, but she did not let those experiences steal her life from her, she decided to leave those experiences behind her and embark on her duty to empower others. Lori has healed herself spiritually and financially and now through her easy step-by-step process, she helps others achieve the level of freedom she now has. Lori's techniques and systems detailed in this book will empower those who embrace them. Lori is here for the long run and I look forward to seeing the success of her clients.

Dear reader, be sure to follow the techniques prescribed here, step by step, move by move, because not only will you regain a different perspective on your story, but will be empowered to thrive in this new global economy. In this new century, we must revive our businesses if we want to stay competitive. Engaging and providing services online is not an option, it is the way our new economy functions. Decide to live life by your own terms. People all over the world, regardless of education, age or gender, will benefit from Lori's method to start a profitable Amazon business. Follow and implement her techniques, they are the absolute truth when it comes to starting an Amazon store. You can live a full, exciting, energized, powerful life of joy owning your own business, Lori skips everything that doesn't work and gives you everything that has worked for her.

LORI DUNHAM

To Your Success,

Eva Maria Barrios

Author, Speaker, Marketer

II.

Introduction

Several years ago, a friend called me one day and said, "I need to find a job, and have no idea how to get started. Can you help me?" I suppose I could say that was my starting point – when I realized my life's mission was to help others take the all-important first step to reach their goals and dreams. I believe that once the first step is taken, one can take the next and the next. Eventually, they will reach their goals. Without ever stepping out, one is guaranteed to never succeed. To me, having knowledge, but not being willing to share it, always seemed to be a waste. To paraphrase J. Paul Getty, "it is better to live off the efforts of many than to work solely from my own". To make this a realization in my own life, I needed to take my own first step and help others, for only in doing so, was I really living my own dream.

Through the years, I have helped many people in a variety of ways, some common, such as resume writing, interview role playing, and job search techniques; and some uncommon, like refining business networking skills, creating fundraising plans, sound-boarding, strategizing elements of start-up businesses, and much more. Recently, a friend called to ask my advice about starting an Amazon Store. She was in the analysis phase of her research where she was weighing the all-important pros and cons. For her specific business opportunity, she would team up with others and, in doing so, a hefty portion of her savings would be required as an upfront investment. Without specifically saying it, I believe that she wanted reassurance that, if she decided to move forward into this new opportunity, she would be able to find success.

Now, success is a relative term, in that, everyone defines success in their own way, whether it be financial inflow, time freedom, accomplishing goals for the future, emotional peace, or the overall elimination of stress and worry. Throughout the conversation with my friend, I began to understand that there are a lot of people who want to start a business, whether it be an Amazon Store or some other venture. They desire to branch out and "do their own thing". They want to find financial security doing what they want and love to do, but, at the same time, want to feel secure that what they jump into will not fail. I cannot guarantee that starting your own venture will ever be easy, painless or even successful – and to do so, would not be ethical. Anyone who wants to start a business venture must have an understanding before ever getting started that the path will have high roads and low roads. To build something amazingly freeing, you may initially work longer and harder than you ever did when working a job for someone else. You may still work a full-time job while building the business in the evenings and on weekends. Because of the decision to "do your own thing", you will miss out on social events that conflict with business needs. You will eventually have to redefine what work-life balance means to you. I can give only one guarantee, and it is this: there are only two ways in which one can really fail at anything – first, by not ever starting, and second, by giving up when the journey gets hard. If giving up seems to be a reasonable solution, it may be necessary to reexamine the reasons why you first got started. I could spend time discussing the importance of "finding your why" in your business, but frankly, there are a host of business mentors that can help with that. Understand from the beginning the reason why you are starting this business, and keep it in front of you all the time. Post it on your wall, your mirror, in your car, or wherever you may see it every day. These reminders will help you find the energy to keep going when things seem hard, or slow-going.

My most rewarding experiences come from following my own life's mission and passion, and that is, to encourage others to take the important first step toward their goal, and then, step back to watch them flourish. What is the first step? It is not so much about action as it is about belief. The first step to achieving any goal or dream is to believe that you can have it, do it, be it, and live it. My joy comes from helping others dig deep to find that morsel of belief and bring it to the surface for encouragement, support and nurturing. I have discovered that there is only one thing that blocks your dreams – You! You are the only one who can stop dreaming. You are the only one who can listen to the naysayers in your head. Sometimes, you can be your own worst critic. So, while you are the only one to block your dreams, you are also the only one who can unblock them by believing that you can have it, do it, be it and live it. You are the only one who can change your life. If you have stopped dreaming, you can start dreaming again – right now. You can have all that you want in life – if you know how to get started. Taking even a single step forward to get started toward your dream moves you out of the realm of dreaming to actually doing.

This book is about how to use Amazon to take the first step – how to start an online store on the Amazon platform. Their business model is one that builds confidence. The skills and knowledge gained from running a profitable Amazon store are transferrable to other ventures. Additional opportunities may also be revealed along the way and you may be able to create multiple streams of income.

It is so important to remember that to succeed, that is, to reach your dreams and goals defined in your own way, or to live out your purpose or life's mission, we all need each other. A common quote from John Donne states, "[We are] not an island..." – no one can expect to achieve their dreams without two things: other people and taking inspired action. It is my hope that this book will be a resource to help you take the first step of inspired action toward your goals. Before moving on into the next chapter, pause for a moment and reflect on what success means to you. Identify specific characteristics of what success looks like. Once you embark on this journey, you will certainly be busy, and one day, you will look up and realize how far you have come. If you already know what your success is supposed to look like, you will be able to recognize your achievements. Once you experience the taste of success, you will be unstoppable. That is my desire for you, for your family, for your life.

III.

First Things First

Now that you are dreaming again, you are ready to take inspired action. Inspired action is where you feel the action in your spirit – you just know it is something you must do, and no matter how you try to ignore it, the feeling keeps coming back. Action without inspiration can lead to frustration and exhaustion. Uninspired action makes you feel like you are spinning your wheels or wasting time chasing things that do not produce the success you truly desire. To be successful with this business model, it is important to recognize from the start that Amazon is a BUSINESS, not a hobby. Certainly, the work can be done full-time or part-time, and can be done from your home, office, car – from your laptop or smartphone – practically anywhere in the world where Internet is available. It is a global business, with global demand, and it should be approached accordingly. When you open an Amazon store, you are the Chief Executive Officer of a company – and there are many decisions and responsibilities that immediately get placed in front of you. While having a business degree is not a requirement, there is an expectation that you can understand the demands that a business will put on you. I am not sharing this with you to scare you – success can be found – but it must be achieved with the right mindset. This business is best run with the characteristics possessed by many successful CEOs – focus, strategy, organization, persistence and determination. The major portion of taking a step toward your dream is knowing that you deserve it.

This business can be very demanding, especially when money and product are vulnerable to timing and vendor requirements. It is best to decide early in the process how you will balance your life around this business. It may not be enough to keep the email inbox organized. The key to keep this business in balance is to maintain inspired action with every decision, and most importantly, build a support team around you – find a qualified and trustworthy housekeeper, chef, babysitter/daycare, errand service and/or personal assistant – or a combination of any of these. Invest in yourself, in your business and make it a priority. It will be hard, but learn early and often to say NO to things that steal your time. Only you can decide what those time-stealers are. You may be in a time-stealing situation when you are doing one thing, but all you can think about is your business; or you are working your business, and feel guilty for not being somewhere else. Certainly, there are elements of absolute balance that are needed to stay physically healthy, spiritually connected and mentally focused, and in those times, you must turn off the business in your mind. You will figure out what works for you – you should if you want to find success. It is very important to understand, and accept, that overnight success is very rare.

To find the life-work balance needed to succeed, you will need the help of a support team over a long period of time.
While this book is suitable for men and women, young or old, regardless of background, ethnicity or heritage, the message specifically for women is to find and adhere to a life-work balance early in the journey. Women tend to carry the responsibility to do things on our own, in our strength, caring for others and putting our needs at the end of the day. It seems as if we have something to prove. But, I am sure that successful women would agree that they did not achieve success alone, and that they had some level of support around them. While it may be nice to have, the support team does not have to be an entire household staff that manages every aspect of your life. A support team can be an amazing assistant who excels at keeping your schedule, and your desk, organized; or as simply as your spouse or family recognizing

and honoring your time to work your business a few nights a week; perhaps your children can spend a few hours with a part-time nanny, attend a Mother's Day Out Program, or go to daycare so you can call suppliers or respond to emails during the day; maybe the neighbor's son can come and walk the dog or take out the trash. There are new online subscription programs that send fresh ingredients to your door, and the family dinner is ready in minutes. There are companies available that you could hire to go pickup groceries that you pre-ordered online and deliver them to you. It will be an initial challenge to decide what tasks can be done by others, and which must be done by you. Accept that others will not get the task done exactly the way you would do it, but, in the end, be grateful because the task is done correctly, and you had more time to build your business. The idea is to understand that true leaders know how to recognize talent and skills in others, and then, delegate that work to them. Understand that delegation is not putting off to others what you do not want to do yourself; rather it is allowing other people to do things for which they are better suited than you are – in a way, you are helping to build their confidence and skills that they need to find the path to their own dream. So, now, let's get started...

IV.

Getting Started

In July 1996, Amazon launched the predecessor "Associate Program", and through the years, it has evolved to what it is today, helping many resellers reach high levels of success. Now is the absolute best time to get started selling on Amazon. Nearly half of every sale on Amazon is split with professional resellers. Professional resellers are people just like you who are selling on Amazon. However, with its rapid success rate and the large number of success stories, there may be a false perception that running an Amazon store is easy — that one only needs to find cheap products (maybe from China), ship items to an Amazon warehouse, and BAM — overnight success! This business is a FAR CRY from overnight success or a get-rich-quick idea. If you are seeking a fast way to quick riches, or perhaps hoping to learn inside secrets to Amazon, this is not the book for you.

This book *IS* for you if you want to learn how to start an Amazon store, focusing on the skills and best practices I found to be useful. When I started my store, I had some paid training, education and mentoring; however, even with that, there were a lot of things I had to learn on my own – the hard way – through trial and error. I experienced financial blows as companies who promised to help me actually stole products from me and charged unnecessary service fees toward my Amazon account. Instead of enjoying the fruits of my labor, I found myself having to "play catchup" during my first peak season. After several months of working hard at the techniques I am about to share with you, I still realized the most-profitable month in sales; however, without the unexpected losses, the month's achievements would have been even greater. Even with the unfortunate events, I became more convinced than ever that getting started was indeed the best decision I ever made.

As I hope you understand by now, my goal is to share knowledge. I am not an attorney or an accountant, nor do I represent any company or government agency. The information in this book is based solely on my experience of starting and operating my own online store based in the State of Texas, United States. Laws in your area may likely be different, so get educated. As you start your journey, you may have many of the same experiences I had, but more likely, you will find experiences unique to you. That is the power of Amazon — no matter your background, education or experience, you can get started, learn this business, and aim for the success you desire.

Because having an Amazon store is a business, it is expected that you will have knowledge of basic business foundations. As you create important documents for your business, be sure to keep the electronic and physical copies in a safe place. If stored on your computer, be sure to back up the files, or store them in a secured location in the "cloud", such as a Google Drive. If you need help obtaining any of the items listed below, please reference the directory in the back of this book.

Create an Amazon Prime® Profile

First and foremost, to begin an Amazon store, you should already have a consumer profile — and even further, that profile should be a Prime® member. A Prime® member of Amazon is a consumer who pays an annual fee of around $100 (at the time of this printing) for special features and promotions, such as free shipping, free Kindle® downloads, free Amazon Music® and many other consumer-facing benefits. Create your consumer profile at www.amazon.com, and then upgrade it to Prime® Membership. You will be prompted to enter your default shipping address and billing information. Having this information stored in your profile will allow for "1-Click" buying from the website, and within other applications on mobile or streaming media devices. Be sure to read all the terms and conditions of having a profile, as well as the privacy and handling of your information. While I have never experienced anything negative regarding my stored information, it is an excellent security practice to change the profile password at regular intervals. If you ever forget your password, there is an automated screening process that allows you to create a new one.

Once you have a Prime® Consumer Profile Membership established, you can now convert your profile from a consumer to a "Professional Seller". Log into your Amazon consumer profile, scroll to the very bottom of the homepage, and under the "Make Money with Us" column, click on "Sell on Amazon". The next screen will allow you to upgrade your profile to a "Professional Seller".

> **IMPORTANT**
>
> Once you upgrade to a Professional Seller account, you cannot downgrade your profile back to a consumer account. The account can only be downgraded to an Individual Seller account. Be sure to read all the details of how to sell on Amazon BEFORE you click the very enticing Orange "Start Selling" button.

If you expect to sell less than 40 items per month, you may sign up as an "Individual Seller". This book is written to help those who will sell more than 40 items each month, and will be considered "Professional Sellers".

For less than $40 a month, plus other selling fees (based on product price, shipping and storage fees), Amazon offers many lucrative benefits that many startup businesses find to be a struggle, such as customer service, shipping, storage, fulfillment, marketing, website optimization, and merchant services. There are also many marketing perks, such as promotional code generation, that become available to professional sellers. We will cover some of these items in this book, but the best source for the latest information is directly on the Amazon website. I will share the names of resources I have used; however, your own research and due diligence is still required before making the commitment to upgrade and start selling.

Upon registering as a Professional Seller, you will be asked to provide a "Store Name". On the Amazon platform, the store name is arbitrary, and serves only as a placeholder for your site within the Amazon web server. Create a store name that suits you, but to keep things consistent, you may want your store name and your legal company name to be the same (more about that in a minute). Also, create a business email address solely for the purposes of communicating with Amazon, suppliers and other persons as you conduct business. It is recommended to create an email address that matches your company name. I use Microsoft's Outlook.com because of its seamless synchronization between my smartphone and desktop for my email, calendar and contacts. Using an email such as fuzzybunnyslippers@email.com may sound cute, but will only be practical if you will only ever sell fuzzy bunny slippers. It is safe to believe that you will want to sell a large assortment of products in your store so you can reach a wider customer base – which translates to more sales, more profits, more supplier orders, and so forth. Customers who purchase your items from the Amazon platform will see your company name and but not your email address; however, you will be giving the e-mail address to suppliers, creditors and other business entities as you build and grow your business. Before getting started, it is important to give your company name some thought and consider a name that leaves an impression, but do not get stuck at this phase. Pick a name that is professional and get moving!

Amazon will contact you through your business email to start the verification process wherein they will request your legal business formation documents, establish your taxing method and validate your business banking accounts for default payments and credits. The list of required documents is not easily found on the Amazon website, in fact, the required documents are unwritten requirements that are disclosed as the process unfolds. To help you prepare and ease the process, I am sharing the list with you in this book. You will want to have all these items readily and electronically available as the request expires rather quickly. If you do not respond, the request could be closed as "unresponsive" and your seller account could be closed. Avoid that hassle by being prepared ahead of time. If you get a request before you are ready to upload the documents, you could determine how much time you are allowed before you must respond, and then two days before the expiration, ask for more time. The response may restart or extend the clock, but there's always a chance that you will not be granted more time. Don't take this specific risk of having your store closed prematurely.

When you start your store, one way to avoid getting "hurt" is to be prepared with all the required business documents BEFORE upgrading your consumer profile to a Professional Seller account.

Seller Central

Soon after upgrading to a Professional Seller, you will receive access to "Seller Central". This is a password-protected back-office website where everything regarding your online store activity or status is conducted. "Seller Central" is a complete database regarding your online store, from inventory levels and bank balances to customer messages and sales reports. This is the place where you will respond to the verification process by uploading your business formation documents. Throughout Seller Central, the help section is interactive based on the active tab from where it is launched. The information and trainings are diverse and in-depth. Seller University is a collection of trainings to help answer common questions about procedures, Amazon policies and algorithmic advice to streamline your store's operations. We will only discuss those topics relative to starting your store, but I highly recommend that you read the information provided – soak it in like a sponge. Seller Central is the main go-to place to keep up with all the moving parts involved in maintaining a thriving business. As with all website-based tools, be sure to protect your password and change it at regular intervals. In late 2017, Amazon implemented a two-step verification process to ensure that the account owner authenticates each user attempting to gain access to your Seller Central. If you forget the password, Amazon has a process to reset it with you.

Due to the global nature of Amazon's business model, the Seller Support team is stationed in various locations around the world. Initial contact is answered via an email to the address in your profile, and all follow-up communications are conducted through the "Case Log" area within Seller Central. If you get into a situation that requires help from the Seller Support team, you can reach out via email or live chat. If it is an urgent need, you could request a callback from a representative. Response times vary based on the issue, but I have found that, although standard issues receive responses that are usually templates or formed answers, when talking to a representative, they are caring and want to help if they can.

I am sure that they receive thousands of calls every day, and issues are repetitive, so when contacting the Seller Support team, ALWAYS be professional in your communications, be specific and use proper business language. Communicate clearly and avoid jargon and inappropriate tone of voice. Start a communication with Seller Support by clicking the "Help" menu and then click the "Contact Us" icon at the bottom of the pop-up window.

When you start your store, one way to avoid getting "hurt" is to ALWAYS respect the Seller Support team regardless of the method in which you communicate with them.

Create a company entity

Amazon scrutinizes their professional sellers to determine if you are a legitimate business. Although there are many aspects not stated as official requirements to upgrade your account to a Professional Seller, I learned that without meeting these requirements, I would have failed the verification process. One such unspoken requirement is evidence of a legally formed business entity, such as a Limited ompany (LLC), an S-Corporation or a C-Corporation.

the store name you select is arbitrary on the Amazon platform, without the legal formation that matches your store name, you may not pass the Professional Seller validation process. If you want Amazon to view you as a professional, then a company entity is a must. It is also a great way to manage tax benefits. A step included in the formation of a company entity is registering your company name with your Secretary of State office. Each state has its own process of registering, but, among other benefits, the basic purpose is to search the records for duplications of your company name in that state, create a state taxing profile, and allow you to eventually request a Sales Tax Use and Resale certificate. The search for duplicate names is only conducted at your state level. To check the availability of your company name on a national scale, you may want to start with the Federal Trade Commission, or contact an attorney familiar with Trademark Law.

I formed my legal business entity using **NOLO.com**. You may wish to contact a professional to guide you in deciding which entity is best for your business, but, in general, if your company will not be going public and will not immediately be offering shares of stock, you could start with Nolo's basic Limited Liability Company Package. Be sure to read all the information on their website, and call them if you have questions. I experienced the customer service representatives to be helpful and friendly. I found the process of completing the LLC questionnaire online to be very easy, quick and affordable. The cost of creating a business entity could be tax deductible as a business expense. Contact a tax specialist who will also ensure that your entity is set up to meet your company's tax goals. If unsure, get tax advice from a trusted professional.

If you are creating a sole-owner or sole-manager LLC, you will need the contact name of a person willing to be act as your "Registered Agent". This person will be listed on record at the Secretary of State as one who can be contacted if you cannot be reached directly. If deemed necessary, the Registered Agent may also receive important business mailings and they should plan to deliver those items to you soon after receipt. The designated Registered Agent must sign an affidavit accepting the responsibility in this important role. The signed document is returned to the Secretary of State, either through the NOLO.com website, or to the company or attorney helping you. The Registered Agent does not have to live in your same town or state. If you use a company or attorney to file your business formation documents, they will likely be the Registered Agent. Regardless of whom you choose, be sure to select someone trustworthy and with whom you have regular contact. If your LLC is a partnership, then either you or your partner can be the Registered Agent on record. There are many companies on the Internet that offer to file for your company, and you may choose whomever you want – just be sure you research them thoroughly and know that you can trust them.

Once you have established a legal company entity, it becomes an asset that can be passed on to your family, or others, as inheritance. It can also be sold to others. It can be a way to help future generations. Be sure to research, or contact an attorney specializing in asset protection to understand how to protect your company if you have plans to designate the company ownership to someone else in the future. You do not have to figure this out to get started; it is just something to keep in mind. When done correctly, your business can be a legacy you can pass on.

Employer Identification Number (EIN)
While you will likely not be employing anyone to operate your online store, creating an Employee Identification Number (EIN) is essential for determining your taxing method with Amazon, opening a business checking account (discussed later), and eventually obtaining a Sales Tax Use and Resale certificate. An

EIN is a 9-digit number assigned to a company entity and is used similarly to how an individual uses a Social Security Number. Obtaining the EIN is free from the IRS and it is easy to apply online at www.irs.gov. The number will be disclosed as soon as the application is submitted, and the EIN confirmation letter can be immediately downloaded. Save this document with the entity formation paperwork. If you would prefer to mail in the application, you can download the form, complete it and wait. The response could take several weeks, and honestly, as an ONLINE business owner, it does not seem logical to apply any other way than on online. **Regardless of how you apply, when you do so, be sure to use the same name as your legal entity, including the "LLC." or the "Inc."** If you use another company or an attorney to file the legal formation documents, they may automatically apply for the EIN as part of the process. If you are using NOLO.com, they may ask to include this service, but I found the process very easy to complete on my own. Remember, the EIN must match your legal entity formation documents in order pass validation with Amazon. Among other things, the EIN identifies your company entity with the IRS for use when filing taxes. In the future, should you hire employees or an assistant, having an EIN is necessary. More information can be found on the IRS website or through a qualified professional.

Business Checking Account

Having a Business Checking Account is another requirement that is not specifically revealed as a requirement to upgrade as a Professional Seller. An advantage of having an EIN for your legally formed company entity is that you can open a Business Checking Account for your company. This account establishes the Business' credit profile. Having a solid business credit profile can help to obtain credit from banks or products from suppliers in the future. Use your formation documents and your EIN to open a Business Checking Account at a bank or credit union of your choice.

I had a "extra" personal checking account that was not in regular use, so initially, I decided to use that account solely for business purposes. I knew it was important to keep business transactions separate from personal transactions, and this account was not in use for any other purpose. I formed my company as a sole-managing LLC where I was the single owner. Since taxes and expenses would flow through to my yearly personal tax return, I thought it would be faster to use the spare account to save time. When the verification process started, I was contacted by Amazon with a message stating simply that my bank account was rejected. They did not indicate a specific reason. After several back and forth email messages with the Seller Central Support Representative, I finally learned that my bank account was rejected because the account statement I submitted during the verification process did not include my online store name/company name – and rightfully so, as it was only a personal account acting as a business account. I quickly located a bank that offered free business checking, had a low opening deposit requirement and that did not charge transaction fees. The first statement was generated 30 days after opening the checking account, and my Amazon status was eventually verified. In retrospect, I see now that I lost 30 days of selling while I waited for my first statement to be generated. Of course, I remained productive in other areas of the business, but until the account verification was completed, I could not sell. The important lesson here is that there are NO SHORTCUTS. I quickly had to get back into alignment with treating this venture as a true business.

When you start your store, one way to avoid getting "hurt" is to understand that there are NO SHORTCUTS. Treat this venture as a business, not a hobby.

Sales Tax Use and Resale certificate

Having this certificate is not so much for Amazon as it is for the suppliers with whom you will obtain your products. As a registered reseller with the State, you can obtain products on a tax-free basis, list them in your store, and the customer pays the sales tax. To use the certificate, present it to a supplier, wholesaler or retailer when you make a purchase. Some will create an account where every transaction is automatically processed as tax-free, while others will request that the certificate be presented with each transaction. At many retail stores, you can go to the Customer Service desk and present the certificate one time. A profile is created into the system which contains your company name and reseller number. In many cases, you may be issued a Reseller ID Card. You can then make tax-free purchases both in the store, and sometimes online. KEEP ALL RESELLER ID CARDS OR CERTIFICATES IN A SAFE PLACE. For safekeeping, I scan my original into my computer as soon as it is issued, and keep physical cards in a card organizer that I carry with me whenever I shop. I suggest setting up reseller profiles with as many vendors as you can as early in the process as possible. Some vendors process the accounts quickly, while others could take some time. You want to be able to take advantage of sales or deals as soon as they are discovered. Time is of the essence in securing products. In the "Supplier Relationships" section later in this book, I will share more information about the resale certificate.

D-U-N-S Number

This is not a requirement of Amazon to become a professional seller; however, because you are treating your online store as a business, it is important to have a business credit profile. Having a business checking account establishes a business profile, but having a DUNS number builds that profile. A DUNS number is provided by a company named Dun and Bradsteet. They operate similarly to the personal credit bureaus, like Equifax or TransUnion, but on behalf of companies. Much like an individual's credit rating is tracked in a profile with the credit bureaus, Dun and Bradstreet creates and tracks a business' credit profile using a DUNS number. This profile is important for building business creditworthiness. Some banks, credit card companies and suppliers may consider this credit profile when deciding to do business with your company. The DUNS number is not used solely for the purposes of Amazon. So, while having a positive business credit rating is essential for working with suppliers, negotiating pricing and shipping terms, the number also affords your company the opportunity to apply for and possibly win government contracts. More information can be found on the Dun and Bradstreet website.

V.

Decide How to Sell

Before you can decide *what* to sell, it is important to first decide *how* you plan to sell. This determination will guide you through how products will be stored and how orders will be fulfilled. Amazon offers two methods: "Merchant Fulfilled" or "Fulfilled by Amazon" ®. Additionally, Amazon allows the sale of products that are described as new, refurbished, used, and collectibles. If you directly manufacture a commercial product, you can develop a Private Label strategy to sell your own products in your online store. While the selling methods discussed here can be switched up with each product you decide to list in your inventory, it may be best to start with one strategy to keep inventory organized and shipping streamlined. After you have mastered the selected strategy, you can then diversify.

People I have talked to about selling on Amazon have revealed a common misconception, in that, to sell products, you must maintain a physical inventory and ship the products to your customers on your own. This method models traditional operations management and fulfillment, to which Amazon refers as "Merchant Fulfilled".

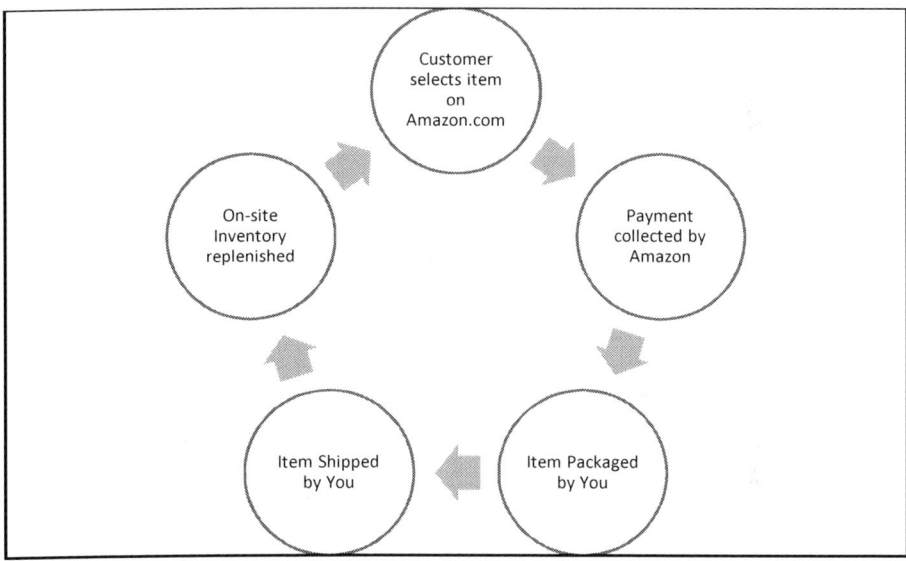

The "Merchant Fulfilled" product lifecycle starts with physical inventory that is stored, managed and replenished by you, or your employees. When a customer purchases a product listed in your online store, Amazon collects the payment and an order fulfillment request is sent to your back-office for processing. You may also receive notification via your preferred method of contact, such as an email or text message. The product is packaged and shipped to the customer directly from your place of business. There is likely local warehouse or storage space being utilized, and shipping is completed via an outside service like the US Postal Service, UPS or FedEx.

There are greater external costs for a "Merchant Fulfilled" strategy; however, it may be a best option for custom-made, antique or fragile items because products of this nature usually generate higher rates when stored in Amazon and have a higher risk of being damaged as it is moved through the large network of Amazon facilities. This is the only selling option available to those who are not Professional Sellers.

As a "Professional Seller", there is another option available referred to as "Fulfilled by Amazon", or FBA®.

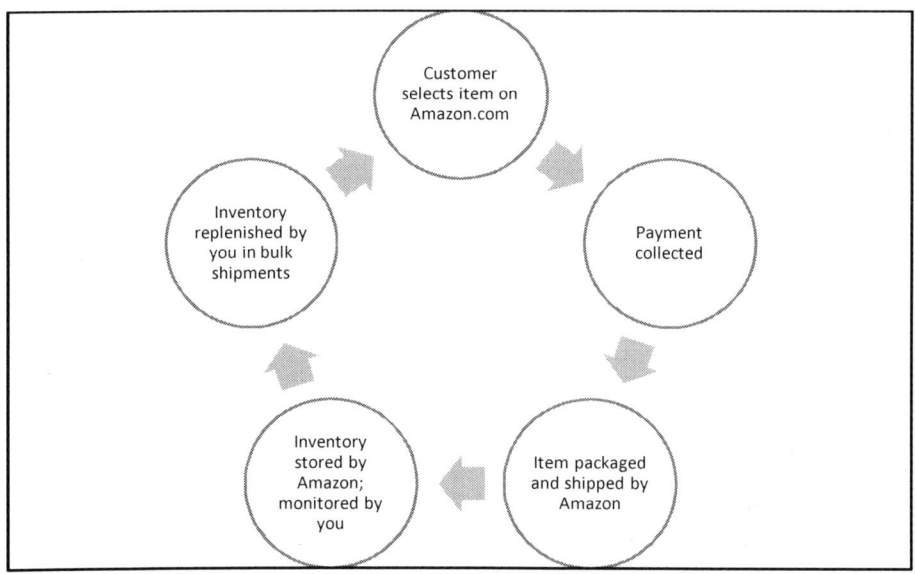

The "Fulfilled by Amazon" product lifecycle starts with physical inventory that you ship to an Amazon Fulfillment Center (warehouse). The products are stored by Amazon, but managed online via Seller Central. When a customer purchases a product listed in your online store, Amazon collects the payment and the product is packaged and shipped to the customer directly from Amazon. A confirmation of the sale is updated in your back-office and sent to your preferred method of contact, such as an email or text message. As products are sold, you can monitor the inventory levels in the back-office. Replenish inventory levels by ordering more products from the supplier, creating the product listings in your online store and sending the items in bulk to the Amazon warehouse for storage. There is no local warehouse or storage space being utilized. When products are ordered from the supplier, Amazon provides instructions as to which designated Amazon Fulfillment Center the products should be sent. Products are likely shipped on pallets directly from the supplier via an outside service like a long-haul trucking company. If smaller quantities weighing less than a total of 150 pounds are purchased, they can be shipped directly to the designated Amazon Fulfillment Center via small package handlers, such as UPS or FedEx. Later, in the "Building Listings and Preparing Products for Sale" section of this book, I will walk you through the steps needed to create a shipping plan to Amazon.

With the "Fulfilled by Amazon" ® method, you may pay suppliers to affix the Amazon stock label to each item, or you may pay Amazon a very affordable rate to label each item for you. Amazon stores, tracks and ships millions of products each year. Your items can be tracked by the manufacturer's UPC, but using Amazon's tracking code, known as an ASIN (pronounced ay-sin), reduces the risk of your product being lost.

There is no exact science as to which fulfillment option will work for you, so after reviewing the storage and shipping requirements, you can decide for yourself. As a general guideline, products shipped to Amazon for storage and shipping are considered "Fulfilled by Amazon" ® and products not stored or shipped by Amazon are considered "Merchant Fulfilled". Both methods can have products listed as "new", "used", "refurbished" or "collectible". When the product listing is created in your store, Amazon will confirm which "condition" is allowed, and if any further requirements are needed before the listing can be completed.

If you manufacture your own product, referred to as "Private Label" you may choose to utilize either fulfillment option, depending upon several factors, such as how your final product is assembled, the requirement for special packaging, the fragility, weight and size of the product and its ability to withstand several moves through the chain of custody, among others. The discussion of the "Private Label" fulfillment is outside the scope of this book because I did not manufacture my own products when I first started my Amazon Store; however, details can be researched online via Amazon and other sourcing websites.

While the external costs for storage and shipping are lower for products "Fulfilled by Amazon" ®, there are added fees paid to Amazon for the storage of inventory and fulfillment of each order. The risk of your inventory "aging out" is greatly reduced. "Aging out" occurs when the costs of storing and shipping a product begins to exceed the cost of acquisition or potential profit. The risk is primarily reduced when products are "Fulfilled by Amazon" ® because they are readily available for immediate shipping. A Prime® consumer has many benefits with Amazon and one exclusive feature is free shipping with delivery within two days. Amazon's determination of where to store popular products based on customer saturation can reduce shipping times. Their massive volume alone generates opportunities for better shipping rates than attempting to improve the rates on your own.

VI.

Choosing Products

Categories

Now that you know *how* you want to sell, next you need to decide *what* you want to sell. Amazon has hundreds of categories. To the consumer on Amazon.com, the top-level categories are listed as "Departments", and clicking on any one will open a myriad of sub-categories.

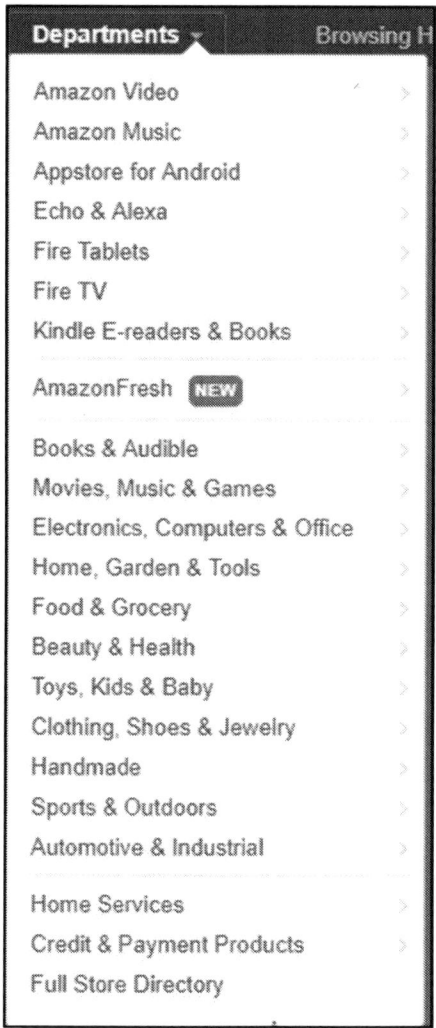

The depth of category specificity that Amazon has created can be mind-boggling. Check it out for yourself by visiting the homepage at Amazon.com.

Products can be listed within a top-level category, but they are usually built into sub-categories several layers deep. For example, "Toys, Kids & Baby" is a top-level category, and sub-categories can go several layers deep to define specific "Toys & Games", such as, Action Figures, Arts & Crafts, Baby/Toddler Toys, Building Toys, Dolls & Accessories, Dress-up & Pretend Play, Electronics for Kids, Games, Grown-up Toys, Hobbies, Kids' Furniture & Décor, Learning & Education, Party Supplies and Puzzles. Choosing any one of these sub-categories will allow the consumer to drill down even further to several levels of specific listings.

To guide the consumer's search through their maze of products, Amazon also posts potential key words under the search box.

It is very important to correctly assign the category to your initial listing. If your product is listed in an incorrect category, the consumer may never find your listing. Thankfully, many consumers search by product name in the main search box, and Amazon shows them all related products regardless of category. Remember, however, that Prime® customers will first only see products you have designated as "Fulfilled by Amazon®".

Deciding which products to sell is first driven by the categories in which Amazon has provided you authorization. Professional Sellers are granted access to several general categories upon opening the store, and other categories need to be opened with further verification. It is through tight monitoring of who sells which products in each category that Amazon protects product integrity and enhances the customer experience. Without the permission to sell in a specific category, you will be unable to list a product in your store. Permissions are requested via a link in the "blocked" product listing box.

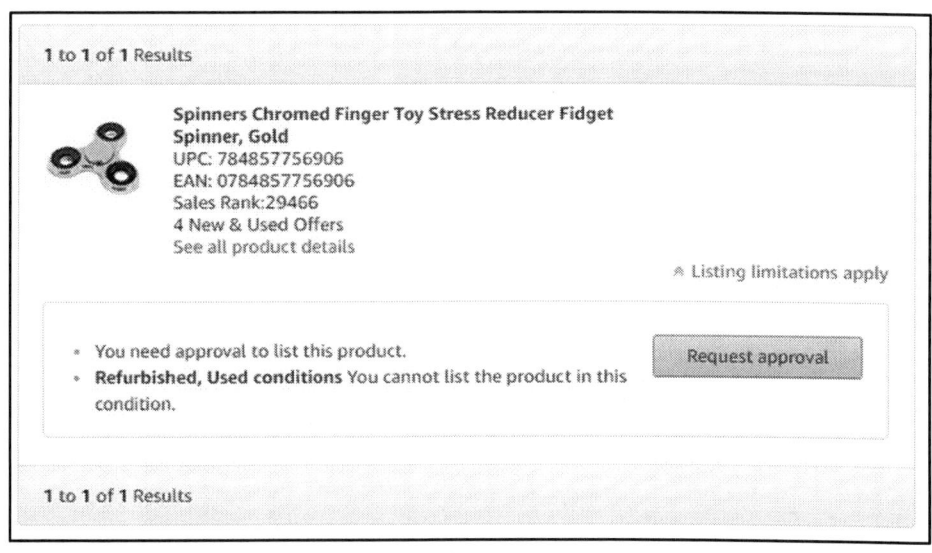

Different products have different requirements to clear the block – or "open the category". To start the process, click "Request Approval". Depending on the product you want to sell, you may be asked to provide an invoice from the supplier

First Step Mentor

Lori Dunham

Don't Go It Alone!

- It's my life's purpose to help you take the first step toward your vision, dream or goal while providing support and encouragement the entire way

- Discuss your vision, brainstorm your best strategy to get started, know your First Steps – all *BEFORE* we work together. Get started with a small $100 deposit.

- I will dedicate 100% of my time to sharing my knowledge and providing insight regarding your goals

- Mutual honesty and open communication is the only way this meeting will work. **I take your trust in me very seriously**

- Additional mentoring sessions are available and terms can be discussed together

- ALL First Step meetings are held in the strictest of confidence. I will not share your information with anyone.

For more information and to schedule a meeting, please visit
www.FirstStepMentor.com

First Step Mentor

or distributor to validate the products are not from yo
or a local garage sale. If attempting to list in a c
category, such as toys and games, you may be asked to provide additional testing affidavits to ensure that the products are safe and align with various government regulations. These documents can usually be obtained from your supplier and are uploaded as .pdf files to Seller Central.

The unblocking process could take some time. It is best to focus on filling product in the authorized, or open, categories, and pursue the unblocking process once you start making a profit. You can begin your hunt for wholesale products based on the categories for which you already have approval. To see which categories you are authorized to sell in, open Seller Central, navigate to the "Add a Product" screen and select the link for "Selling Application Status".

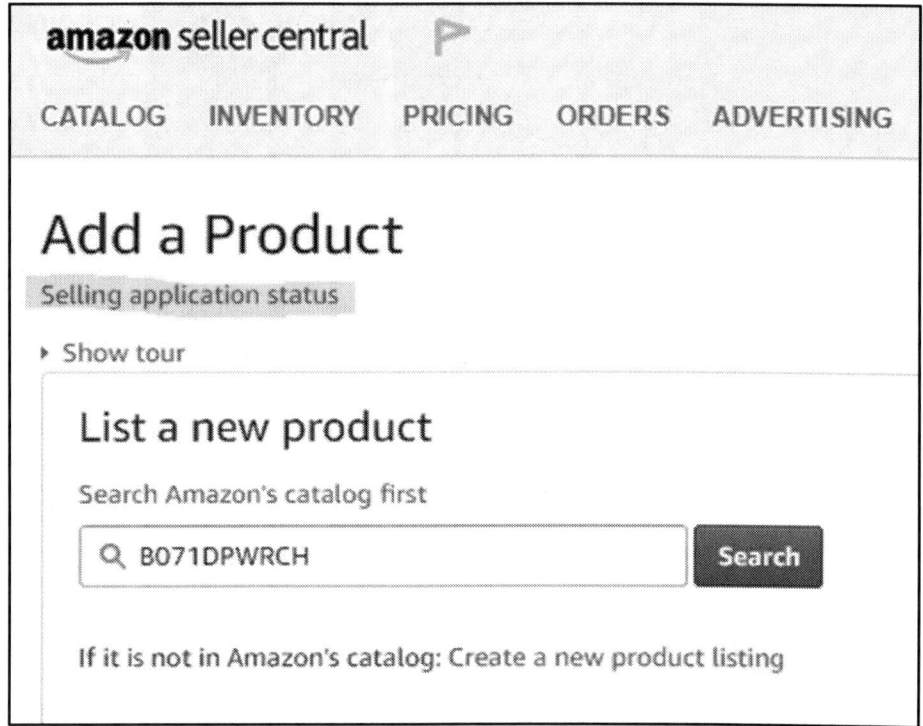

I learned this the hard way. As a Professional Seller, I was granted several open categories upon starting my store. Instead of ordering and shipping in products that I knew could be listed and sold immediately, thereby generating quick revenue and building confidence, I pursued the process of opening as many categories as I could. At the time, I thought that this would allow me the opportunity to order a greater range of products, and possibly larger orders, from my supplier. I thought that the supplier would look more favorably upon my company if the orders were larger. The unblocking process took nearly 2 months – and in some categories, I am still waiting (at the time of this writing). In the meantime, adding to the delay of presenting by business bank statement, I was now the proud owner of a store with no product. The result was that I was paying Amazon the monthly fee for the store "presence", but had zero sales for nearly the first 3 months. Additionally, I learned that my suppliers were delighted to do business with me, regardless of my order size. Their goal is to sell product through honest channels, and while larger orders are always welcomed, they treat all companies (their customers) with the same level of professionalism.

When you start your store, one way to avoid getting "hurt" is to load your inventory with sellable products in categories where you are already approved.

Let's Do the Math

Math does not have to be a four-letter word when it comes to Amazon. The Seller Central is full of reports that analyze sales, fees and profits. There are tools that analyze a given profit position compared to weekly, monthly and yearly figures.

Basically, Amazon does most of the "heavy lifting" after the sale is made. However, cost is certainly a huge factor when considering which products to sell, including wholesale costs charged by the supplier, warehousing or storage costs whether the product is stored at an Amazon Fulfillment Center or in your business space, and shipping costs both to Amazon for bulk shipments and costs to ship the product to the customer. However, cost is not the only consideration when deciding which products to sell, and it is important that you analyze the pre-listing numbers to determine if the product is a good choice.

An important analysis is that of Return on Investment (ROI). I found this to be the single most important calculation because it is a figure that remains stable among several scenarios. The outcome is presented as a percentage, so whether the calculation is conducted on a single item, an entire case, or potential sales for an entire month, the ROI percentage remains the same. The ROI is the percentage amount of profit you can expect after all costs have been considered in relationship to the selling price of the product. I allocate an estimated 25% of the selling price toward shipping, storage and processing fees. (This may seem high, but it is only a generalization, and can be adjusted to fit your specific goals.) I personally shoot for no less than 65% ROI, but you could potentially accept lower based on your specific goals. With a 65% ROI, when the product sells, 100% the investment made to secure the product is realized, along with an additional 65% revenue. **The ROI is calculated by dividing the estimated revenue by all the calculated costs.** I usually base the percentage on a monthly sales volume, but it could also be determined for a single item, or a minimum order quantity imposed by the supplier.

Let's look at an example.

I found a 7", white, ceramic flower vase on a supplier website. The minimum order quantity was one case of 24 vases. The wholesale cost of the case was $48; thereby the wholesale cost for a single vase was $2. I researched the product on Amazon and found that this single item sells for $19, with estimated monthly sales of 288 units. Based on this information, how can I quickly know if it is a good "deal"? Initially, it seemed like a good "deal", but it is better to have a strategy where I can know for sure. First, I can evaluate the deal based on an individual unit, or one vase. Second, I can base the "deal" on the minimum order quantity, or one case of 24. (Since, in this example, I'm not able to buy a quantity less than the minimum, this may be the best method). However, the third option is to evaluate the "deal" based on how many units are expected to sell in a single month, or 288 units. If I believe I could sell 288 units in one month, I could order 6 cases at one time to save money on shipping. This savings will ultimately be an indirect reduction to the 25% fees, and an increase to the per-unit revenue. This fluctuation is the main reason that using an ROI calculation will save a lot of time. And as we have discussed, time is of the essence when analyzing a product for your store.

In this example, $19 selling price times 25% for monthly costs is $4.75. What this calculation shows me, is that, for every $19 sale, I can expect fees of $4.75, leaving potential revenue of $14.25 per vase. These figures are all potential, best-case scenario, and they can fluctuate depending on what strategy you are using (an individual unit, minimum order quantity or monthly sales), but the ROI remains the same.

	Potential Revenue	Wholesale Cost	ROI Calculation
ROI Based on Individual Unit (1)	$14.25	$2.00/vase + $4.75 fees ($6.75)	2.11 or 211%

ROI Based on Case or Minimum Order Quantity (MOQ) (24)	$342	$48.00/case + $114.00 fees ($162)	2.11 or 211%
ROI Based on Expected Monthly Sales (288 units or 12 cases)	$4,104	$576/12 cases + $1,368 fees ($1,944)	2.11 or 211%

Remember, that while the ROI calculation is more stable than recalculating for fluctuating prices and fees, it is still only a guide, not a rule. Considering our goal of 65% ROI or better, this would be a great "deal". Now, the decision lies with which quantity to purchase first – 1 case (minimum), 12 cases (match expected monthly sales), or somewhere in between. Regardless, because of the stable ROI figure, you now know it is a profitable move.

One final thought about the ROI calculation is that it can also help gauge the lowest selling price to remain profitable. If you want to remain competitive with other sellers, you need to act fast to reduce our price when the selling seasons are at their peak. It will save a lot of time later if you calculate your "lowest selling price" when you are analyzing the "deal". Using the above example, if you desire a 65% ROI, as you can see, the figures have well exceeded that goal. Recalculate the ROI formula and you will be able to determine your lowest selling price. Many of these calculations can be formatted in an Excel spreadsheet, so tweaking numbers becomes very easy.

ROI is only one of several considerations when deciding if an item is right for your inventory. Other factors to consider include Product Ranking, Number of Product Stars and Reviews, and Days to Replenish Inventory. You can find a product's ranking, number of stars and product reviews by scrolling to the bottom of the product information page.

Product information	
Product Dimensions	3.6 x 3.5 x 0.5 inches
Item Weight	2.4 ounces
Shipping Weight	2.4 ounces (View shipping rates and policies)
Domestic Shipping	Item can be shipped within U.S.
International Shipping	This item can be shipped to select countries outside of the U.S. Learn More
ASIN	B071DPWRCH
Item model number	NK690699
Manufacturer recommended age	5 years and up
Best Sellers Rank	#29,466 in Toys & Games (See Top 100 in Toys & Games) #35 in Toys & Games > Novelty & Gag Toys > Novelty Spinning Tops
Customer Reviews	3.3 out of 5 stars · 38 customer reviews

Let's discuss each of those factors now.

Product Ranking is specific to Amazon where, based on sales volume or popularity over a pre-determined amount of time, a product "rests" among others in its main-level or sub-level categories. A Ranking of 10 – 10,000 is a good mining area for products.

At first blush, many new sellers will buy into the buzz and target the Top 10 selling products on Amazon. However, these items are so popular that their inventory levels are hard to maintain without buying and shipping in massive quantities. While it is not impossible, for a first-time seller, especially one with a limited budget, it is difficult to achieve. The goal is start smart – without getting hurt – and start with inventory that is easy to obtain and quick to sell. This will establish favorable inventory and sales levels within Amazon. When inventory levels are low, or fluctuate erratically, Amazon considers that when rating your store. The instability over time could result in a poor rating. Also, products in the Top 10 are usually branded, meaning that, special approval from the brand owner is required before the item can be listed for sale in your store. Approvals could take time to obtain, but are usually granted to sellers with a strong track record and high store rating. Do not be discouraged! There are thousands of items that rank from 10 to 10,000, and many are very profitable. In due time, as you become better acquainted with the processes and work steadily to be efficient, your sales will increase, inventory will stabilize, and your store rating will be set organically. Bottom line: focus on what you can do, and the rest will happen on its own. Eventually, you will be able to tap into the Top 10 products. Remember, the goal is to learn without getting hurt.

Stars and Reviews are used by many online platforms to rate a consumer's experience with a product and service, such as TripAdvisor, Yelp! and others. Amazon uses this information a bit differently to ensure that the consumer has an exceptional experience from the moment they begin searching the Amazon.com website. Amazon uses feedback to determine the rank of a product in a category, and subsequently the overall account health of a seller's store. Products that achieve 4 or 5 stars for a product, and at least 50 (preferably good) reviews, is a good product for consideration. These are guidelines, not the rule, so you could consider products that do not meet these criteria – just do so with caution, and be sure to evaluate if the time spent on analysis will result comparably in a sizeable profit. Remember, you are the CEO of the business, and decisions that lead to success, or failure, belong to you.

While the Cost, ROI, Ranking or Star parameters are not likely to align perfectly on each item under consideration, a product that meets 4 or 5 of the criteria is certainly a top-choice. Products with 3 aligned parameters could be carefully considered if there are no other viable options. In each case, weigh the matched parameters very heavily when deciding to purchase the items. Having slow-moving products stored for a long time in an Amazon warehouse could potentially increase indirect costs and negatively impact overall profitability. Products with less than 3 matched parameters should not be analyzed further.

When you start your store, one way to avoid getting "hurt" is to consider products with minimums of 65% ROI, 10,000 Ranking, 4 Stars and 50 reviews.

VII.

Where to Get Products

The three most popular ways to secure products for your store come from Retail and Online Arbitrage, direct purchase from suppliers (wholesalers, distributors and/or manufacturers) and drop-shipping. The purchasing strategy you decide to pursue will determine the type of product you want to list in your store. It is important to understand that not all products have to come from overseas to be profitable. In fact, there are hundreds of profitable options within the US. I am not opposed to obtaining products from outside North America; however, for beginners, it is best to reduce the potential hassles of importing. The time will come when you are able to branch out to use these options.

Retail and Online Arbitrage is defined by locating and purchasing a product from a retailer, either in the store or online, at a low price and selling it in your store for a higher price. It is the purest form of capitalism, and although a heated topic of debate, it is perfectly legal. You can find products on clearance or through advertised sales promotions. You can also source products from stores that offer overstock, buyouts, unclaimed merchandise, auctions or buyer returns. When conducting any arbitrage activity, be sure to focus on departments in which you are already approved. Open categories are called "ungated"; restricted categories are called "gated". For example, if a store is having a sale on beauty products, but this specific category is not open to you, or "gated", you will not be able to create the listing. If you buy product in a category gated on Amazon, the listing cannot be created. You will have to find another outlet to resell your products. It is not impossible to find another platform, but those strategizes are outside the scope of this book.

The Amazon Seller App, available as a free download for Android and iPhone, is a password-protected mobile connection to your Seller Central. While not all the features of the full Seller Central site are available in the app, there are many great features that are only available in the app. The app is especially helpful when shopping in a store as it allows the seller to scan a product's Universal Product Code (UPC), a small, black and white barcode that is recognized by inventory and point-of-sale devices and databases universally.

Scanning a product's barcode will display the product's current listing price on Amazon.com, as well as the ranking, stars and reviews that we discussed earlier. The app will also provide the expected Amazon fees imposed should you decide to ship it in for the "Fulfilled by Amazon®" service.

Further, if the parameters and fees align with your specific goals, the app will allow the seller to create the FBA listing in your store's inventory – immediately and on the spot. The item will not show as available for sale in your store until the item is shipped into the Amazon warehouse, but your inventory listing will be created. Keep in mind that the app creates listings only as "Fulfilled by Amazon®"; however, the data of the product can still be useful to analyze if the product is worth the purchase.

When sourcing products online, the app is not as useful because you can have your Seller Central website open in a separate tab in your Web browser. All the comparative information is available on the Amazon website. Additionally, I found the Chrome browser to work the best.

Items that require special handling or packaging, are fragile or too heavy to ship can, and should be, listed as MF (Merchant Fulfilled). This will save money on the extra shipping costs to get it to the warehouse and reduce the risk of damage during transport between and storage in the Amazon various warehouses. To help with creating the inventory listing, any product that you want to sell can be created in the app as "Fulfilled by Amazon®" while at the store, and then, the listing can be changed to Merchant-Fulfilled directly in the Seller Central website when you are ready. Any items that you want to store locally and ship only when an order is made, should be changed to a Merchant-Fulfilled listing. Remember, however, that Prime® consumers will not see your Merchant-Fulfilled listings, so you may have to implement extra advertising tactics to draw shoppers to your listing. Consider those costs against the apparent savings, and make the decision that is right for you.

After scanning an item in the app, or entering the product's UPS into the Amazon search bar, you may find several listings for the same UPC where the item is bundled in quantity multi-packs, such as a pack of 2, 8, 16, etc... The idea behind a UPC is that it is designated specifically to a single item; however, because sellers of all types are creating listings under the same UPC, the search may yield several listings. Don't let this confuse you. Just find the listing for a single item and do your comparison based on that listing's data.

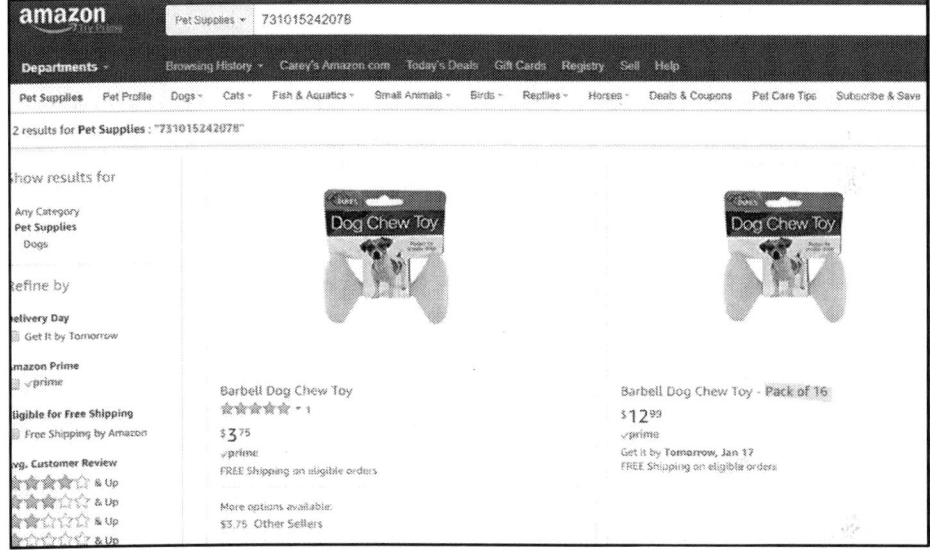

Supplier Relationships

A **supplier** is defined as a company that provides products to resellers. Suppliers can be either manufacturers, wholesalers or distributors. Manufacturers make the product directly, and then authorize distributors or wholesalers to resell their product directly to the public on their behalf. The manufacturer provides the product to the wholesaler or distributor directly at low, below-retail prices. Rather than selling directly to the public, in many cases, a distributor, will sell to wholesalers, and wholesalers then sell to resellers. A reseller can be a retail store, an online presence or both. The reseller displays or posts the products for sale. If there is no designated distributor, the reseller can buy directly from the manufacturer.

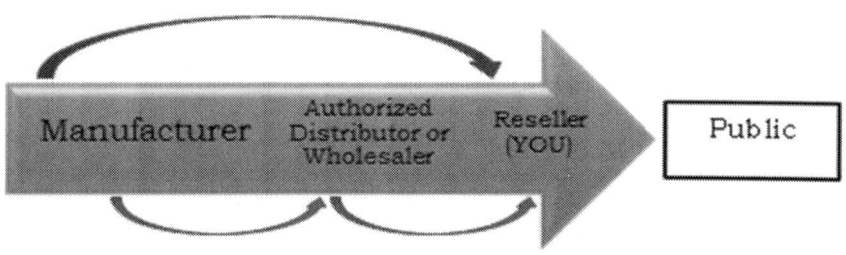

Where the manufacturer usually focuses on a select line of products that target a specific consumer, the Wholesaler will usually have a variety of items available. Wholesalers can also have established relationships with manufacturers from overseas, so you will not have to manage the hassles of importing. The item and where it is made will determine with whom you will create a relationship.

Having business relationships with several suppliers is highly recommended; however, forming a solid relationship with a select few quality suppliers in the beginning is the key to finding in-demand products at a reasonable cost. Be sure that the supplier offers a variety of products at wholesale costs. If the supplier can offer direct shipment to an Amazon warehouse, all the better (more on that later).

Drop-shipping

Many sources on the Internet teach that drop-shipping is the best way to get started. Drop-shipping is an agreement between the supplier and the reseller where the product is stored at the supplier's location and shipped directly to the consumer on behalf of the reseller once the consumer places an order. This is taught as a great startup strategy because there are no or low upfront costs and products do not have to be stored locally or at Amazon (therefore eliminating storage costs and the Amazon selling fees). I am not opposed to this strategy. If utilized properly, it can help boost online sales. I see this as a good strategy for Merchant Fulfilled listings on Amazon, or on other online platforms. However, if using this strategy with Amazon FBA, it is important to understand that your store's ranking is determined by speed of fulfillment, customer satisfaction and feedback. When an item is drop-shipped from the supplier directly to your customer, you are dependent on the supplier's performance to keep your store ranking healthy. Additionally, all aspects of the customer experience are directed to you – all the customer service inquiries, returns and refunds — will flow to your inbox. If you have a team in place to manage inquiries from around the world, every day, all day long, then this is a wonderful strategy. If not, however, understand that Amazon will not be concerned with the reasons as to why a supplier failed to perform, or if you wanted to step out of the office to get some sleep — they will hold you solely accountable. Over time, if your store continues to perform fulfillment services poorly because of an inefficient supplier or inadequate resources, your store could be shut down. Remember that Amazon's sole focus is on the customer's experience — and it must be highly rated.

When you start your store, one way to avoid getting "hurt" is to delay in using the drop-ship strategy until you develop a strong store ranking, build necessary resources and strong supplier relationships.

When establishing a relationship with a supplier, you will want to obtain the products tax-free because you are reselling the items directly to the public (consumer). Amazon will charge the sales tax to the consumer's order, and indicate the amount on your sales reports. When it is time to file your sales tax report to the State Comptroller's office, you record the amount of sales tax collected by Amazon on your behalf. Contact a tax professional for more details regarding the tax rate and tax law requirements in your state.

A Sales Tax Use and Resale certificate, sometimes referred to as a Resale Certificate or a Tax-Exempt Certificate, is issued by your State Comptroller's Office and is used to validate your company as a reseller when obtaining a product from a supplier. Manufacturers will keep a copy on file for all future orders. Wholesalers and distributors may or may not ask for a copy, if they know in advance that you plan to resell their items on Amazon. A retailer – either in the store or online – will request a copy of the certificate, and may issue you a Reseller ID card, or simply provide you with a reseller number. This card, or the number, may be requested upon checkout, with or without a cashier. If you do not present the Reseller ID card or number upon checkout, you will be charged sales tax for the order. If this happens, you may claim the amount when you file your sales tax report, and the amount is deducted from the amount expected from your sales. There are some tax calculations involved, so if this happens, be sure to get proper guidance from a tax professional.

To prepare for all the possible situations, obtain a Resale Certificate as soon as possible. Depending on your state, you may be able to apply online. After establishing an online profile, for which you will need your Filing number with the Secretary of State and your EIN from the IRS, you will be prompted to complete a short questionnaire. Be sure to keep all the contact information consistent. The certificate is mailed to your main company address within 2-4 weeks, depending on your location.

When you start your store, one way to avoid getting "hurt" is to obtain a Resale (Tax-Exempt) Certificate and establish reseller status with multiple retailers as soon as possible.

VIII.

Building Listings and Preparing Products for Sale

This section is the most active when preparing your items for sale on the Amazon platform. As mentioned above, the Seller App can build a listing in your store when you are on-site at a store, and the barcode is scanned. This only creates a portion of the listing, and details must still be completed in the Seller Central website. We will walk through the process of creating a new FBA listing in the Seller Central website so you can understand all the components. Then, if you use the Seller App, you will understand which pieces are completed automatically.

When an item is listed in your online store as "Merchant Fulfilled", it will not be immediately viewable to a Prime® customer. Based on a customer's search criteria and their type of membership, that being either Prime® or non-Prime,

Amazon ranks the products first by "Fulfilled by Amazon®", then Prime® designation, then the price of the item, among other filters. If a product has the same previous criteria, Amazon will display the listings based on store rank. The higher the rank, the closer to the top of the display page the listing will appear. The top listing, known as the "Buy Box" is a coveted section of any listings page because the consumer's eyes are directed to that listing, which is perceived to be their best option. I would certainly guess that nearly 100% of sales are selected from listings in the "Buy Box". It is for this reason, among others, why the "good health" of your store is so important to maintain. If your product is not "Fulfilled by Amazon®", or not a Prime® product, it will fall to the bottom of the search results. Unless a customer is either savvy enough to define the appropriate filters or diligent enough to search all the pages in the search results, you take the risk of your product never being selected for purchase. Deploying marketing tactics, such as sponsored ads, could bring your listing into the view of the consumer, but those techniques are outside the scope of this book.

As mentioned earlier, Amazon offers a paid service that will "hire" Amazon to affix their tracking label, known as a FNSKU, to each FBA items shipped to them. The cost is comparatively low and worth the investment.

Building an FBA product listing in Seller Central

Analyzing the products offered by your chosen supplier is a hefty undertaking. Suppliers offer hundreds of products, and to analyze all of them would take an incredible amount of time. There are two best practices I recommend when processing data from your suppliers. First, create a spreadsheet that includes columns for each of the comparative parameters we discussed earlier, as well as columns to the net cost, potential ROI, and potential profit. Second, it is best to know in advance what departments you want to stock in your store. You could make this decision based on an upcoming season. Because of shipping and processing timelines, it is best to source and order products based on an advanced window of three months out. For example, in November and December, instead of analyzing products that are Fall or Holiday related, shift your focus and search the offerings for products related to consumer activities anticipated in early January through March - within the next three months.

Let's stop for just a moment and consider what activities happen in the first quarter (first three months) of the year. In January, people make New Year's resolutions – be more active, lose weight, and possibly travel more. You could stock your store with fitness equipment, luggage and travel accessories, or any related items. In February, people tend to prepare for Spring with home improvement or DIY projects of all kinds. You could stock your store with hardware, tools, supplies and equipment. In March, there are preparations for Spring Break, new gardening projects, and sports activities start to gear up. You could stock your store with gardening tools and gadgets and sports equipment. What other activities or consumer behavior can you think of that occur between January and March? What are some things you tend to do during this time? If you need help, conduct some research online, look at a wall calendar to see the days designated to a certain activity or group, or ask some friends. Based on the conclusion of your research, decide which products you will analyze. Remember, while you are getting started, to only focus on obtaining products in categories where you are ungated.

When you start your store, one way to avoid getting "hurt" is to analyze your supplier's products with an Excel spreadsheet to avoid manual re-calculations and focus your analysis on "ungated" products that will be in demand at least three months away.

Narrow your items to analyze to around 250-300. From this grouping, approximately 100-150 will fit your desired parameters, and even fewer may be allowed as listings in your store. Those that "make the final cut" should be considered for an order with your supplier.

5 Steps to build an FBA Listing

NOTE: Staying idle on any one screen for a lengthy period of time will freeze the process. The screen may need to be refreshed, data or options may need to be re-entered, before moving forward. Be sure to have all your information readily available so that the page does not time out. There is not usually a notice or pop-up message to confirm the page is frozen, so you may experience a delay in your cursor's response.

Step 1 is to determine if your product is in the Amazon Directory. Log into Seller Central, click on the tab labeled "Inventory", and then select "Add a Product".

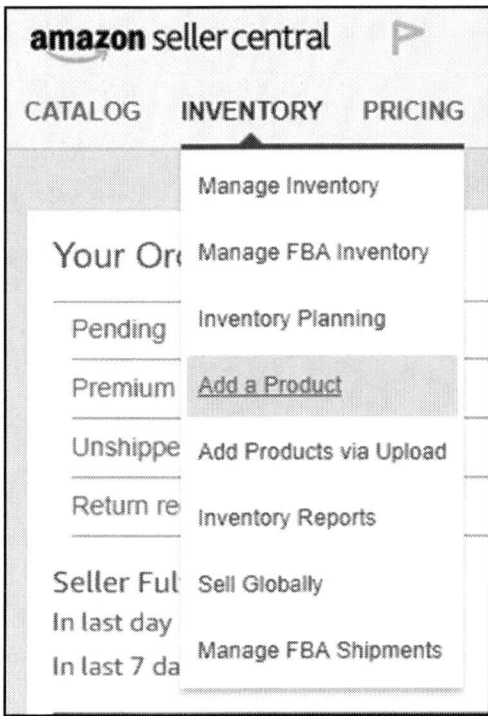

A new window will open where you can enter either the product UPC or the Amazon ASIN number.

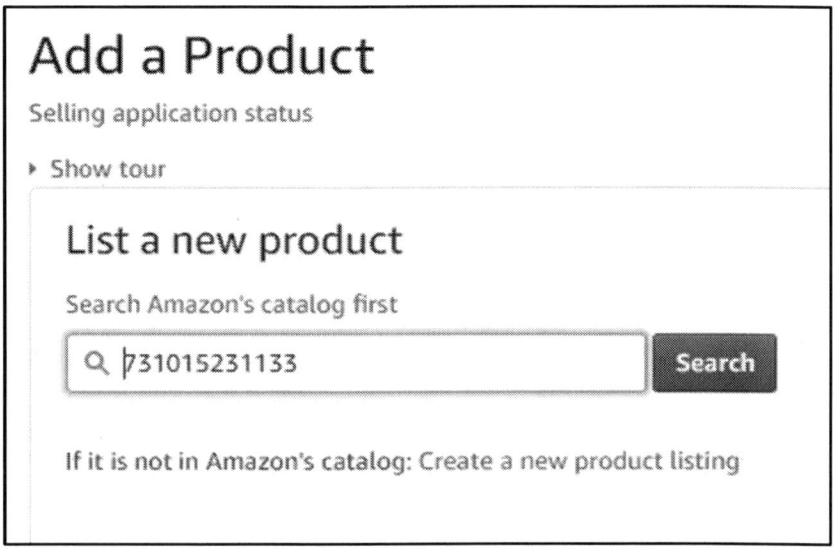

There is some heated debate among some resellers as to whether "tagging onto" an existing listing is ethical since the listing was created by a different seller. If you really feel strongly about it, could click the link to "create a new listing". Before you do; however, understand that Amazon allows and encourages your offering to be "tagged" to an existing listing because it keeps the consumer's search results succinct. Imagine hundreds of search results for the same product – the pages of search results would be huge. Also, creating a new listing may place your item at the bottom of the search results, even if it is Prime®, because of the ranking of the product. A new listing will have no sales history, no ranking, no reviews and no stars; therefore, based solely on rank, it will be at the very bottom of the search results. Having multiple sellers "tag" their offerings to an existing listing is not a problem as Amazon maintains ownership of inventory levels of a specific listing based on the store name and other criteria. This concept stems from the idea of the UPC – your listing promotes an individual UPC and the quantities are managed by Amazon.

When I create my offerings, I look for an existing listing to use. It must match my product 100% - including brand name, quantity, color, and UPC. If ANY part of the existing listing is different from the physical product you intend to list, then, a new listing MUST be created. For example, a UPC pulls up a blue cup, and it is the same brand, dimensions and quantity that I am purchasing from my supplier – but I have a red cup, instead of blue. If the existing listing has a variation button, click that matching variation and build the listing based on that product page. If there is no variation button, determine if the existing listing has a disclaimer that multiple colors are available. In this case, the color choice is not available to the consumer. They will get whatever color arrives randomly. This is fine for some items, like toys or gadgets, but for furnishings, appliances or tools, expect to see the variations button.

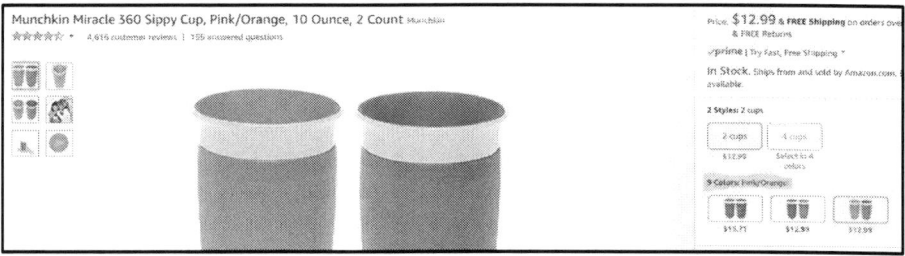

On the chance that there is no existing listing, I move onto to the other selected items on my supplier's list. I may come back to it later, or if I have enough products to list, I may leave it for another time. Deciding to bypass an item without an existing listing is purely a choice. Keeping in mind that the new listing may not be available in the Buy Box, or even land on the first page of the consumer's search yield, it is best to determine if the effort is worthwhile in this stage of learning. There will certainly be plenty of opportunities to build new listings, but the immediate goal now is to get up and running as fast as possible – without getting hurt.

Once the UPC is entered into the "Add a Product" search box, the Amazon Directory will show all the possible matching items. This will bring up all the items that match the UPC number you entered.

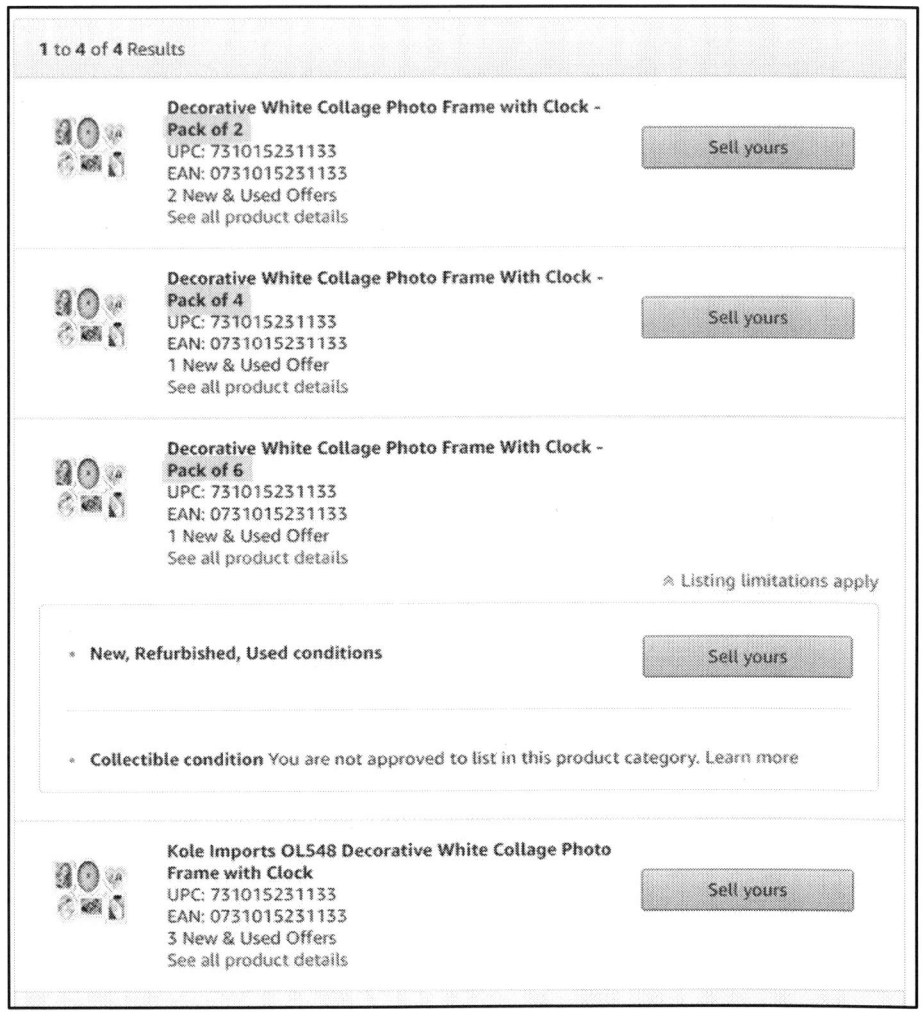

In this example, one UPC is created for four listings – the first three are for multi-packs, and the last is for a single item. In some cases, the listings that are displayed may be for completely different items altogether. In these cases, select the one that matches your product quantity.

In contrast to the concept of a UPC, where a UPC is designed to relate strictly to one variation of a product, the Amazon Directory will show several variations because inexperienced sellers are listing multi-packs under the UPC for a single item. While we cannot change entries in the Amazon Directory, it is important to build our listing correctly when we are the first to do so. The product's UPC is assigned by an outside governing agency, not by Amazon.

If a listing does not include the UPC you entered, try entering the ASIN in the "Add a Product" search box.

To find the ASIN, you may need to research the item on the main Amazon website and view it on the product details page. To find the ASIN, open www.amazon.com, and enter the product's UPC in the main search bar, and hit Enter. When the product information page is displayed, the ASIN can be located in two places. The first place is easiest to find but could be hard to detect. Look in the URL and find the ASIN – usually starting with B00 or B01:

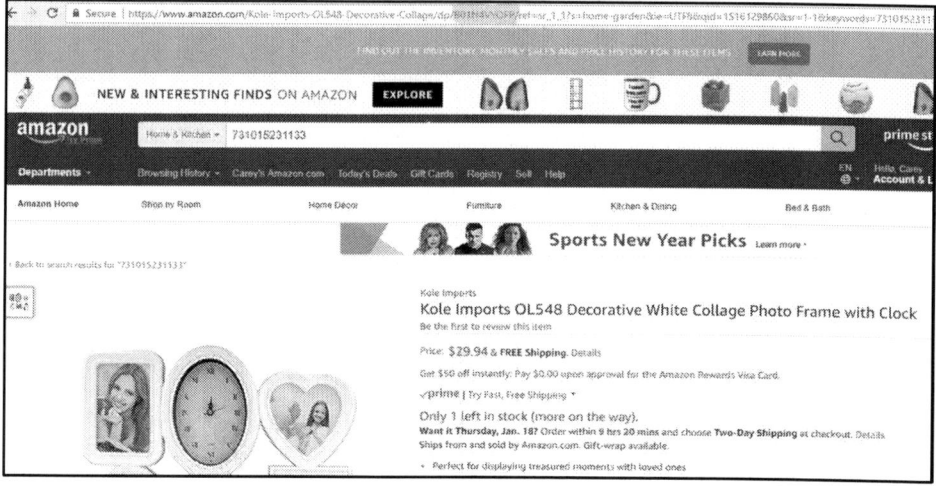

The second place to locate the ASIN is in the product's Information section, located at the bottom of the product listing page:

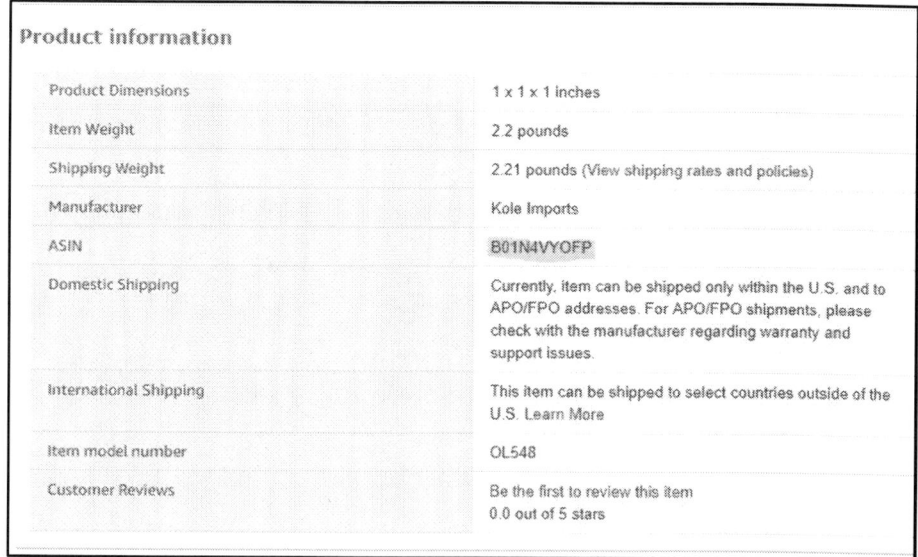

Once you have located the item you would like to list, click the "Sell Yours" box next to the item.

Step 2 is to enter your "Offer", which includes your product sales price, condition and method of fulfillment.

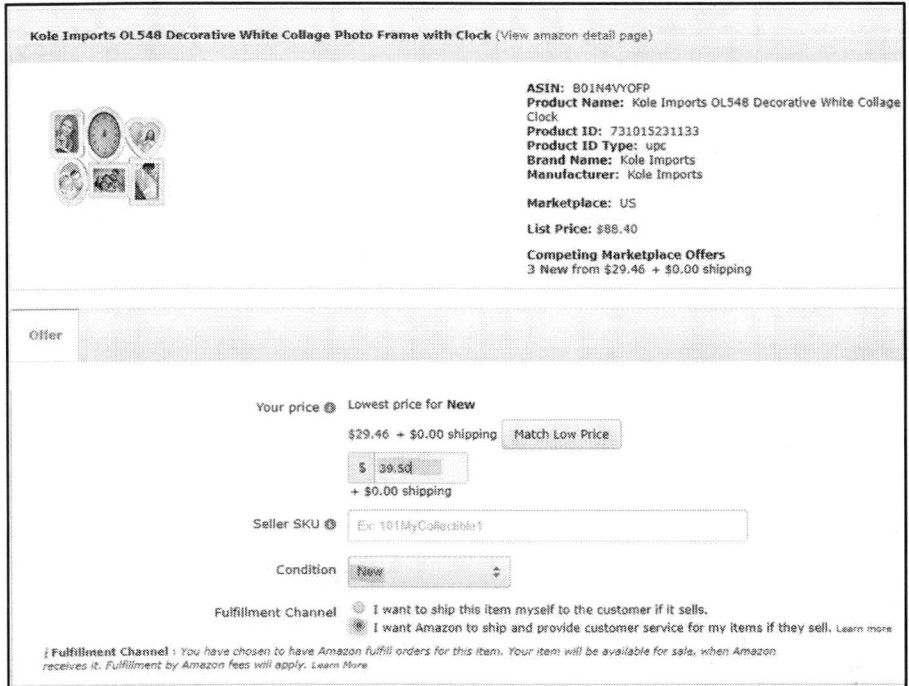

When building the listing for the first time, enter a price about $10.00 higher than the price listed on the Amazon website. For now, this price is a placeholder until your items are received by the Amazon warehouse. It will be changed later to a competitive price for the Buy Box.

From the dropdown menu, select the condition of your item. Because we want to implement the fastest way to get started, without getting hurt, focus on listing only new items regardless of which type of supplier you choose. Items that are used or refurbished can be listed, but there are more risks and potential problems.

Over time as you build your inventory, or if you decide at some point to list private label items, the Seller SKU can be used to track those items. Since you are just getting started with new items from a manufacturer, the Seller SKU is an optional field. When this field is used, it is unique to the listing and cannot be duplicated in other listings. This restriction is something to consider when you contemplate using this field in the future.

Select the second radio button to indicate that you want Amazon to fulfill the product orders for this item – this is "Fulfilled by Amazon®". You may notice that there is an "Advanced" button that is closed. The information on the Advanced screen is optional and used to enhance your listing – especially when it is private label or merchant-fulfilled. If you are fulfilling via Amazon, information on the Advanced screen is not needed. When the offer is complete, click "Save and finish".

Step 3 determines how Amazon tracks your product once it arrives in the Amazon warehouse. Track by "Merchant ID" or "Amazon Label" are the only two options offered. Sometimes, only the "Amazon Label" is offered. Regardless, always select the "Amazon Label" to ensure that your product is tracked accurately in the Amazon database. By selecting this option, your item will require an Amazon FNSKU label to be applied to each item shipped in. The FNSKU is used to track the location of the item within the warehouse, and if lost or damaged, eases the search process.

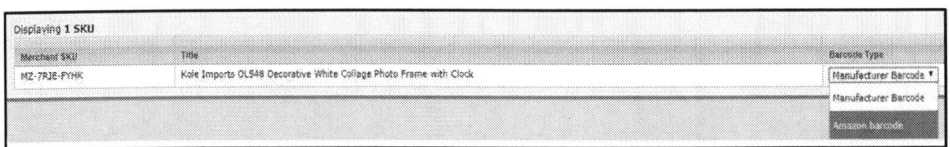

Additional details regarding the importance of using the correct barcode type is provided at the top of the screen. Refer to the information for more clarification.

Step 4 is fairly new, and it gives resellers the opportunity to notify Amazon if a product is hazardous or dangerous in any way to the employees or consumer. While hazardous and dangerous items are not banned from being sold on Amazon's platform, special provisions are required to ensure the safety of Amazon's employees and the product as it traverses the many routes to the customer.

Condition	Item exceptions	Required information
NewItem		⊕ Add dangerous goods information

Press "Add" and a new popup screen displays the required questionnaire.

While the answers may seem trivial, be sure that you read this page VERY CAREFULLY and FULLY UNDERSTAND what items are considered hazardous and dangerous. You may be surprised to learn which common items are considered. If you do not declare an item as hazardous or dangerous by error or omission, you risk having your store shut down. Amazon takes this questionnaire very seriously.

If you have a product that meets these conditions, you may proceed with the listing by answering "yes" to the appropriate questions. Answering "yes" will prompt additional questionnaires to complete the listing.

START YOUR OWN AMAZON STORE

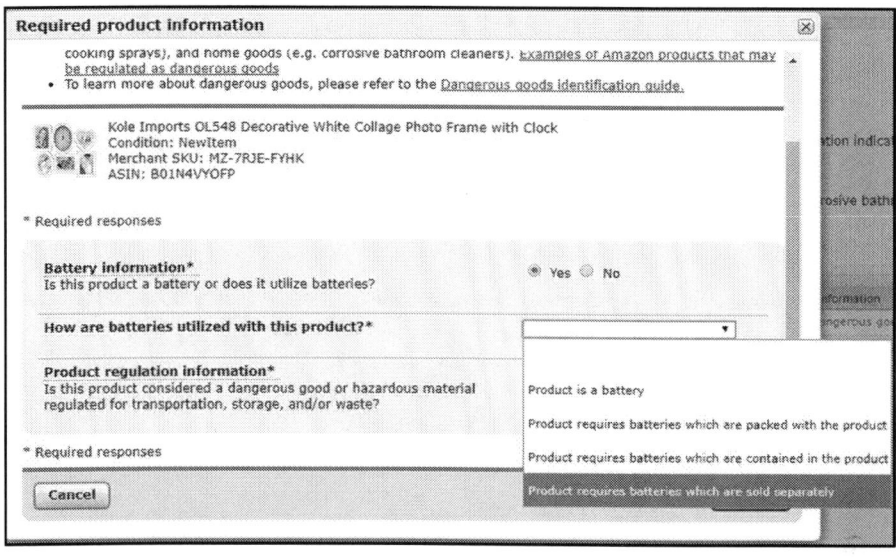

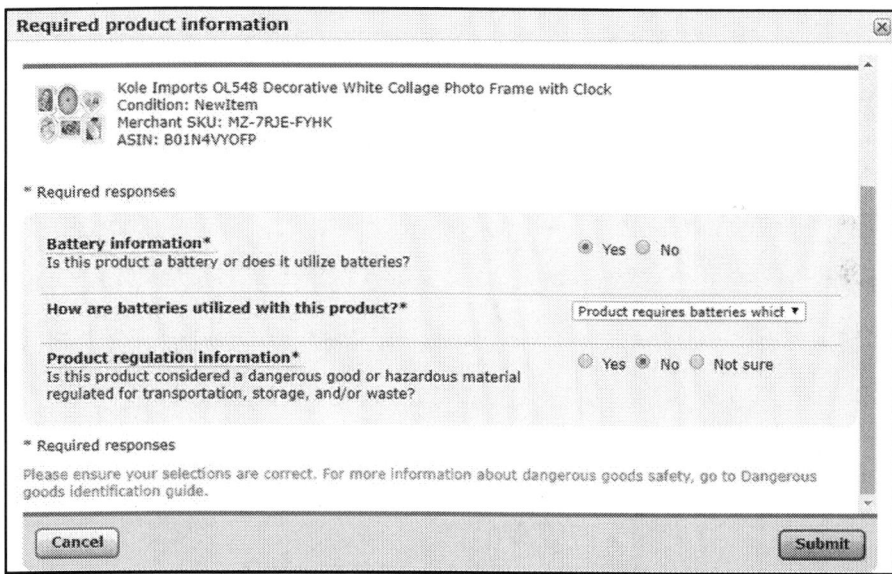

In some cases, additional storage fees may be applied to items considered as hazardous or dangerous. When possible, especially when starting out, avoid listing items that are hazardous or dangerous. If something should go wrong, you will be held responsible, and it is a risk too great for a new seller to absorb. Keep this in mind when finalizing your list of products from your supplier. When the questionnaire is complete, click "Submit", and then "Save and Continue".

When you start your store, one way to avoid getting "hurt" is to avoid selling items that are considered hazardous or dangerous. While you may eventually reach a point to sell items in this category, the risk is too great for a new seller.

Step 5 confirms the details of the listing. If you forget to provide details, or if information entered is incorrect, **click the "BACK" arrow at the bottom of the window.** DO NOT USE THE BROWSER BACK BUTTON – this will knock you out of the store, and you may have to start all over again. If you confirm the listing, press the "Confirm and List" button.

5 Steps to build a Merchant-Fulfilled Listing

The previous steps followed to build an FBA listing are also followed for building a Merchant-Fulfilled listing. Once the listing is posted in your Inventory screen, click on "Edit" and select "Change to Fulfilled by Merchant".

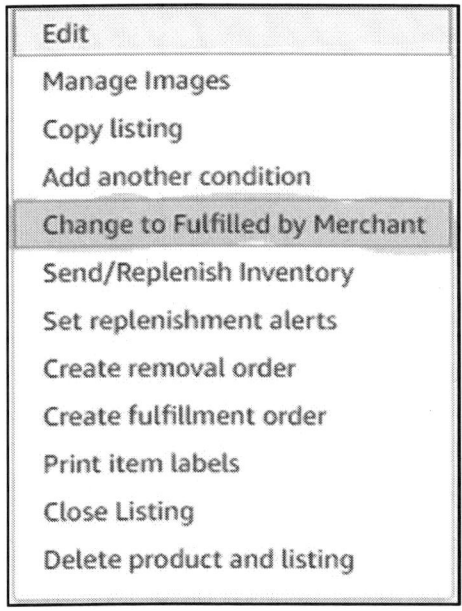

To view only Merchant-Fulfilled listings, you can sort your Inventory at the top of the Inventory grid.

Before you select this option, let's review the important key differences in service:

1 – You are responsible for shipping the product to the customer within the defined terms of the listing. If you do not account for the correct amount of shipping for the product,

you will absorb the extra costs. For example, if you list a product that includes delivery within two business days, but the customer selects overnight delivery – and the overnight fees are not calculated correctly – you will absorb the difference in costs between two-day and overnight service.

2 – You are responsible to store the items outside of Amazon, and the condition must be protected. Therefore, if you list an item as "New", you must ensure that the product is protected and stays in "New" condition.

3 – Depending on how much product you actually have on hand, you may need to purchase outside storage space. To determine if this is a good business decision, compare the monthly costs of renting off-site storage versus the Amazon selling and storage fees. It is important to note that while the off-site storage solution may seem reasonable, consider that the Amazon fees are only applied when the items sells. If you have space in your home or garage to safely store and protect products, you may be able avoid off-site storage costs for a while.

4 – Merchant-fulfilled listings may not be displayed to Prime users if they are savvy with applying search filters. Therefore,

your product could take longer for customers to locate, if at all.

5 – Because merchant-fulfilled products are ranked lower in the search results, you may have to incorporate outside advertising strategies to draw an audience to your listing.

6 – Merchant-filled listings are best for products that are fragile, heavy or that require special handling or extra preparation. Products that meet these conditions incur extra charges by Amazon, so managing the shipment of these products on your own will ensure the tender-loving-care that only you can provide.

In either case, if the details of the listing are incorrect, or more fields are needed to make the listing more appealing, you can make changes to the listing through the "Edit" button in your inventory screen.

Remember, these changes are not made just for your offering, but for everyone using that listing. So, you could be helping someone else sell their product – if their price is lower, ranking is higher, and so forth. From my experience, I have come to understand that there is certainly enough room for everyone on the Amazon platform. So, if you see a listing that needs correcting — either the descriptive fields or the category is incorrect — take steps to make the corrections. This helps you, as well as the other sellers, but overall, it helps Amazon remain a place where offerings are precise and of high-quality. In the end, this ensures a positive customer experience.

When you start your store, one way to avoid getting "hurt" is to help the Amazon community by correcting listing errors. If your product is sharing the Buy Box with Amazon, NEVER undercut Amazon's price.

Your listing is now complete, and the item is shown in your inventory. If you selected to build a listing that is "Fulfilled by Amazon®, the next screen will prompt you to start a Shipping Plan. If the item was Merchant-Fulfilled, this screen will not appear.

NOTE: Once an item is added to your FBA Inventory listing, the listing is not deleted, even if the fillable quantity lives at zero.

Create a shipping plan

Creating a shipping plan takes concentrated effort as a lot of information is gathered to notify Amazon's employees about the expected shipment, the shipping costs to send the products to Amazon, as well as, to calculate warehouse space required to house your products. If you are creating a listing in your inventory and then immediately building a shipping plan, click "Create a shipping plan". The current inventory item will be added to a new shipping plan.

Sequential steps will move you through the process, depending on your answers. Missing any important details can cause unnecessary delays, expenses or lost shipments. I will highlight the aspects of each step that can sometimes go unnoticed. Remember, detail is key.

Step 1 – Creating a new shipping plan

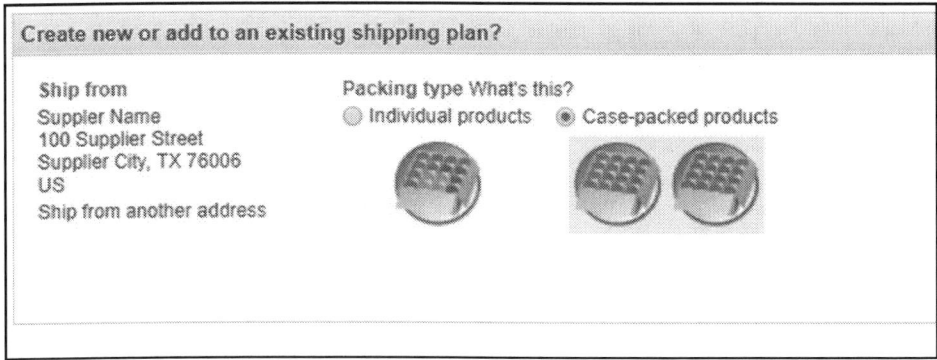

Ensure that the "Ship From" address correctly reflects the Supplier's warehouse address. When working with a sales or account manager at the Supplier, their office address may not be the same as the warehouse, so be sure to ask specifically for the warehouse address. In future screens, you will also need the warehouse contact person's name, email and phone number. The warehouse address is where the transportation company will go to pick up your products. The last warehouse address used will be listed automatically. To change the address, click on "Ship from another address." The next screen will allow you to save several addresses for future use.

"Packing Type" will prepare the Amazon employee's expectations of what will be received. "Individual products" are smaller quantities of various products and all are placed in the same case. "Case-packed" products are one specific product (one UPC) and multiple quantities of the same product are in the case.

For example: Individual products could be 12 gadgets, 6 figurines and 6 thingamajigs in the same box. Case-packed products could be 24 gadgets in the same box. In both instances, you can have multiple boxes.

In instances where you are sending products directly from your supplier to the nearest Amazon warehouse, select "Case-packed" products. When you've selected the correct option, click "Continue to shipping plan".

Step 2 – Setting the Quantity

To continue with the shipping plan, you will need packaging information from your supplier. For each item that you are shipping, you will need to calculate the total units to ship.

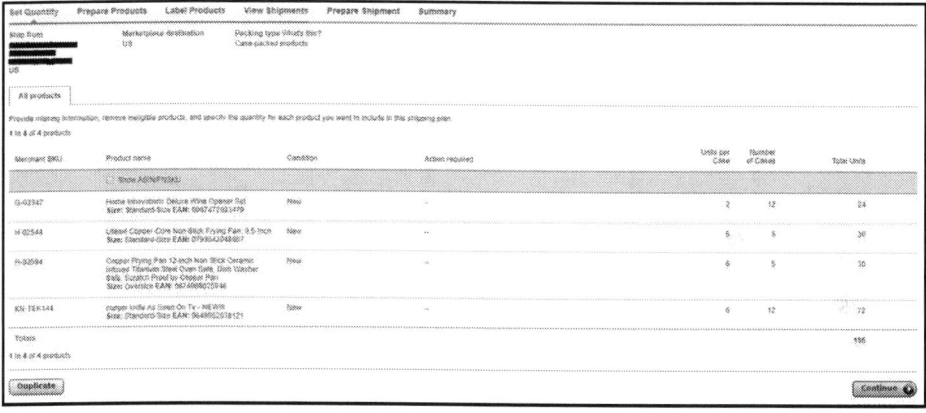

Step 3 – Preparing the Products

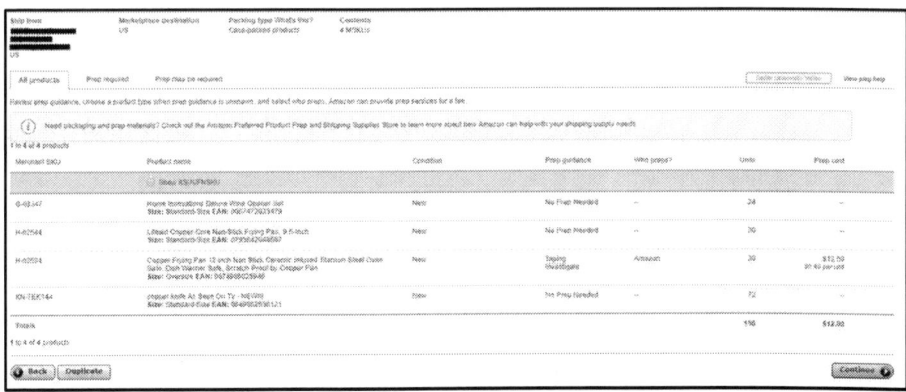

From the next dropdown menu, "Prep Guidance", select if any type of preparation needed. This selection tells Amazon if the item needs extra packaging or larger cartons to fulfill an order. Depending on the item, the supplier and/or the costs, you can determine the best source to provide the extra packaging. In many instances, no preparation will be needed. If your item does not require any additional packaging it can be shipped as is, for example, if a board game is already wrapped in cellophane, select "No Prep Needed" from the dropdown menu.

Some instances will require extra preparation, for example, fragile items may require bubble wrap, upholstered items may require poly-bags, apparel may need special handling before the item can be moved to its storage shelf or shipped to the customer. Products must be packaged so that they can withstand transit and can be safely handled by our associates.

Either way, it is necessary to identify who will "prep" the products – either Amazon or the You/Supplier. The dropdown box advises Amazon if they will need to provide this extra packaging, or if the supplier will send it already wrapped.

In those instances when Amazon will prepare the item, additional prep costs will be calculated and displayed on the screen. When all preparation assignments have been completed, click on "Continue".

To have Amazon prepare your products upon receipt at the warehouse, you must first enable "FBA Prep Services" in the Main Settings menu. You can also choose who preps your products by default in your FBA settings page. Changing the default does not affect previously created shipments or any prep preferences you have defined for specific items.

NOTE: Planned preparation or the application of the ASIN label by Amazon may delay the full receipt of your shipment; however, unexpected preparation may cause further delays in the completion shipments being received – sometimes by as long as up to 48 hours.

Step 4 – Labeling the Products

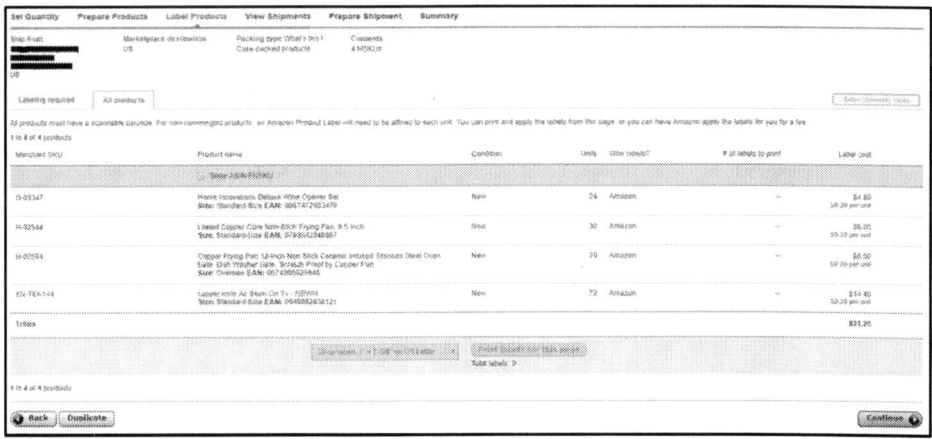

This option defines who will apply the Amazon Barcode (ASIN) label required on each item being fulfilled by Amazon. As you may recall, Amazon offers a service called "Fulfilled by Amazon". One of the benefits of this service is that the receiving team at the Amazon warehouse will affix the ASIN label for you. The label will be placed on each product that will be available for sale from your inventory. This ASIN label is used to track your products as they move throughout the fulfillment process. The costs for this service are minimal and the fees are deducted from your Amazon account (or credit card on file) when the shipment is sent to the customer.

While the Fulfilled by Amazon service is convenient, you may wish to inquire with your supplier if they can affix the labels as well. Some suppliers have the capacity to do that, while others do not. If they do, their costs may be comparable to Amazon's fees. Determine which cost is better and, on this screen, indicate who will apply the label.

When "Merchant" is selected, the ASIN label must affixed to each item BEFORE it is shipped into the warehouse – either by you or your supplier on your behalf.

An estimate of the FBA Prep Fees based on the expected preparation services for the selected products is provided for each item on the shipping plan. All costs for Amazon services will be calculated and totaled at the bottom of the screen. Be sure each line item shows an estimated Amazon labeling fee. If this amount does not populate automatically, the page may need to be refreshed, and the Amazon Option may need to be selected again to show the amount.

If services are performed by another party, the costs will not be calculated here. You will need to obtain and pay for those services outside of Amazon. When ready to move forward, click "Continue".

NOTE: Be sure to select the appropriate labeling party for EACH ASIN listed. Depending on the speed of your computer's processor, there may be a slight delay, and the screen will briefly refresh after each change, so be sure to go slowly and double-check each line before moving forward.

Step 5 – View Shipments

Once all the products are entered into the shipping plan, and the quantities, prepping and label costs are calculated, Amazon will show a designated warehouse code to where the individual cases or pallets should be shipped. Pay close attention to how the quantities are split up. Amazon determines, based on storage and sales volumes, among other variables, where items should be shipped so that the customer's orders are shipped from the closest warehouse. If a customer is a Prime ® customer, the item must to available in close proximity to the customer's address to allow for fast delivery – usually within 2 business days. This speed of delivery must also occur without incurring excess shipping costs for Amazon. As you can imagine, Amazon's shipping volume has resulted in deep shipping discounts with multiple carriers. Centralizing items based on previous and forecasted sales demand and product availability helps keep costs low and operations efficient. Depending on these and other variables, you may see one shipment or many. Once the shipping plan is complete, click "confirm".

Checking and double-checking may seem trivial, but I assure you that getting it right is very important to reduce confusion, and extra charges. Refer to the Product worksheet that was created during the chapter where we discussed "Choosing Products". Add a column to that worksheet and record the Shipment ID next to each item in that specific shipment. You could later sort the worksheet by item, and it should mirror the shipping plan. Having the Shipment ID documented will become helpful in the future, because, when Amazon notifies you of the shipping status, they will reference only the Shipment ID.

At this point of creating the shipping plan, each separate shipment will require specific shipping information. It is important to double-check the contents of each shipment. To do this without impacting the shipping plan, click on the "Download SKU List" to open a text file (.txt). Confirm the details of each item.

```
FBASCB86Y4 (2) - Notepad
File Edit Format View Help
Shipment ID    FBA5CB86Y4
Name    FBA (10/30/17 12:54 PM) - 2
Plan ID PLN151DF6F
Ship To Amazon.com.dedc LLC, 2700 Center Drive, DuPont, WA, US, 98327-9607
Total SKUs       1
Total Units      18
shipment-total-cases    3
Pack list       1 of 1

Merchant SKU     Title   ASIN    FNSKU   external-id     Condition       Who will prep?  Prep Type       Who will label? Units per Case   Number of Cases Shipped
H-02594 Copper Frying Pan 12-Inch Non Stick Ceramic Infused Titanium Steel Oven Safe, Dish Washer Safe, Scratch Proof by Copper Pan
B01K9ESLUC      X001L2PEX2      EAN : 0674986025946     New     Amazon  Taping  Amazon  6       3       18
```

Properly packaging and preparing units helps to reduce delays in receive time, protect your products while in our fulfillment centers, and create a better customer experience. If any changes are needed, NOW is the time to make changes. Close the text file and click on "Work on Shipment".

Make any necessary changes in the steps previously discussed and navigate back to this screen.

Step 6 – Prepare Shipments – Small Parcel or LTL

If you are shipping contents less than a total of 150 pounds, you will likely prepare the shipment for delivery by UPS or FedEx. This type of shipment is called "Small Case". You can send several small cases, up to 50 pounds each, to the Amazon warehouse at one time, but each case will have its own shipping label and unique tracking number. For contents greater than 150 pounds, or 10 or more cases on a single pallet which total 150 pounds or more, the shipping plan will be created for a trucking company. This is known as "LTL" shipments. Once the supplier's warehouse picks your items, they will send you a shipping manifest to confirm the best method of shipping. If they will use pallets, they will stack the pallet(s), and confirm the height. As a rule, pallets are usually 48" x 48" and no more than 6' high. You can send multiple pallets to the Amazon warehouse at one time, but each pallet will have a unique set of four (4) labels applied to the outer sides of the shrink wrapping.

From the shipping plans already created, click on "Work on Shipment" to continue.

Step 6a - (UPS/FedEX)

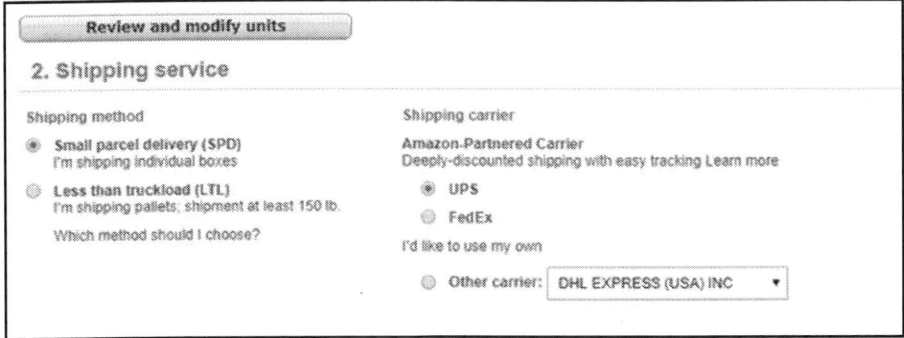

When shipping your items in separate boxes, under 50 pounds, select the SPD option, and then select either UPS or FedEx. Later, you will calculate the shipping costs, so if the costs seem high, return to this section and select the other carrier. I have found FedEx pricing to be lower in many instances but check them both for yourself. For the best pricing, always use an Amazon-Partnered Carrier because the rates are ridiculously low – average is calculated to be about 50 cents per pound. Selecting a non-preferred partner may not provide the deep discounts that have already been negotiated by Amazon. This discount only covers the costs of shipping to an Amazon warehouse. Codes are printed on all labels to provide information about the product, the preparation needed, the store owner's name and inventory levels.

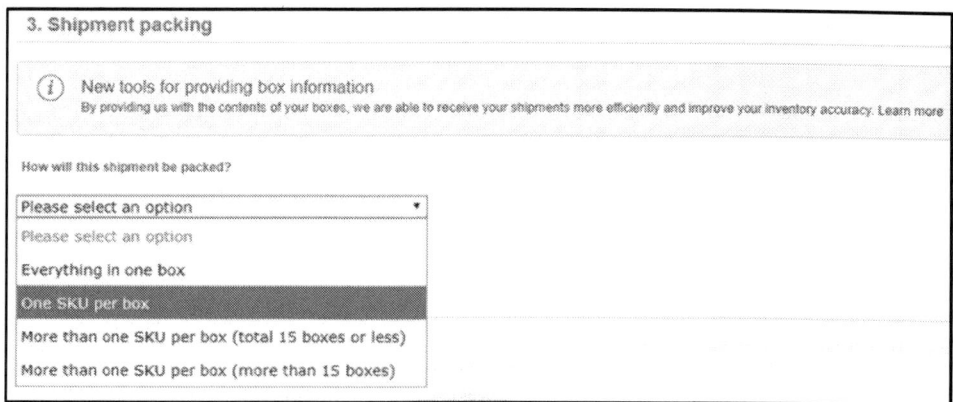

This section determines how many shipping labels to create. As described earlier, select the appropriate option for how your products are stored in the boxes.

Next, you will enter the carton dimensions – this is the Length x Width x Height of the box (case) that holds each product. Also include the case weight. If you are sending a partial case, calculate the actual dimensions and weight of the items being shipped. This information is available from your supplier. While most suppliers know that this information is needed, and will have it readily available, some suppliers will need to conduct research to find it. You may pause the working of the shipment until you receive the information. Once you receive it, you may add the information and continue. While waiting for the supplier's information, the shipping plan will be in "pending" status. Suppliers usually ship cases of the same product (same UPC) in larger quantities depending on the size of the item.

Once you have entered all the required information, ensure that the case pack quantities (number of items in the box) and case quantities (number of actual boxes) correctly total the number of items being purchased from the supplier. This number is very important because it will be used by Amazon's employees to compare the physical count of the items upon receipt at the warehouse. If the physical count does not match the shipping plan, this data will help in the investigation to find the missing items.

It is important to note that a case pack is not the same as a multi-pack. Case packs are intended to be split, and the contents sold individually. Multi-packs are sold as bundles or sets. A case pack may be sold as a multi-pack but must be prepared according to the requirements for products sold as a set.

NOTE: For case-packed products, you must remove or cover any scannable barcode on the case itself. Only the individual items inside the case should have scannable barcodes.

4. Shipping charges

You are responsible for providing accurate shipment information and for the actual cost of the shipment. Providing inaccurate infor

Shipping carrier	# of boxes	Shipment weight	Billable weight	Estimated shipping cost
UNITED PARCEL SERVICE INC	1	45 lb.	45 lb.	$15.50

☑ I agree to the terms and conditions **Accept charges**

Indicate that you agree to the terms and conditions, and accept the shipping charges for the carrier previously selected. To review the terms and conditions, click the blue words to open a pop-up window. If the estimated shipping cost is too high, return to Item 2 on the screen and select the other carrier. If you change the carrier, you may need to re-enter the case packaging, dimensions and weight again. Take a screenshot of the previous information to help speed up the process. When you're satisfied with the shipping charges, click "Accept Charges". These fees will be deducted from your Amazon seller account (or credit card on file).

Step 6b – LTL Shipments

When shipping your items in multiple boxes or on pallets, where the entire shipment is over 150 pounds, select the LTL option. As the shipment will likely be coming from the supplier, the shipment contents will likely be packaged as one SKU per box.

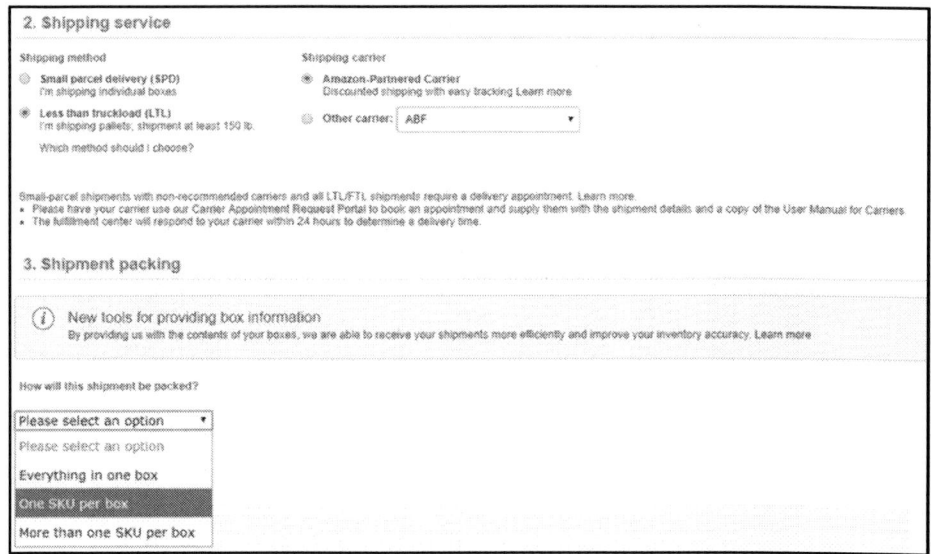

While there are two ways to upload pallet data for LTL shipments, the best way for beginners to complete this task is with the built-in Web Form.

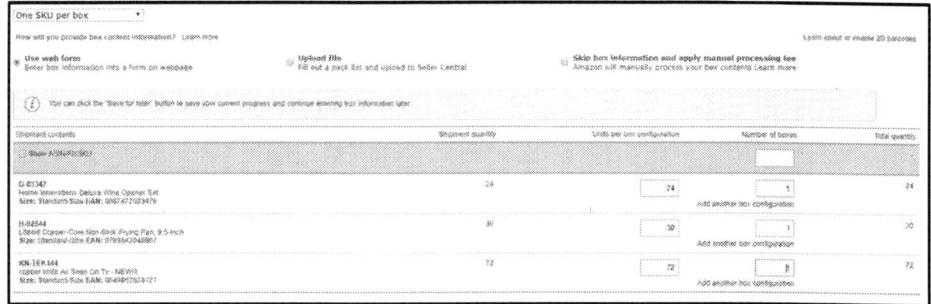

Select the Web Form option and enter the quantities of each product – just like in the SPD screen. Remember that the case pack quantities (number of items in the box) and case quantities (number of actual boxes) correctly total the number of items being purchased from the supplier. This number is very important because it will be used by Amazon's employees to compare the physical count of the items upon receipt at the warehouse. If the physical count does not match the shipping plan, this data will help in the investigation to find the missing items.

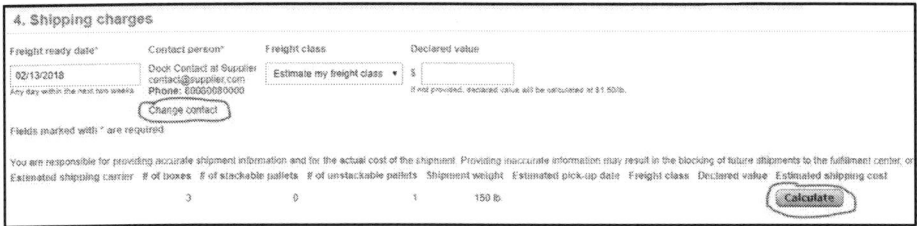

Ensure that the warehouse contact person's name, email and phone number is correct. This is the person with whom Amazon and the carrier will coordinate pickup of the pallets. An appointment is usually scheduled to ensure efficiency, so communication among the parties is vitally important.

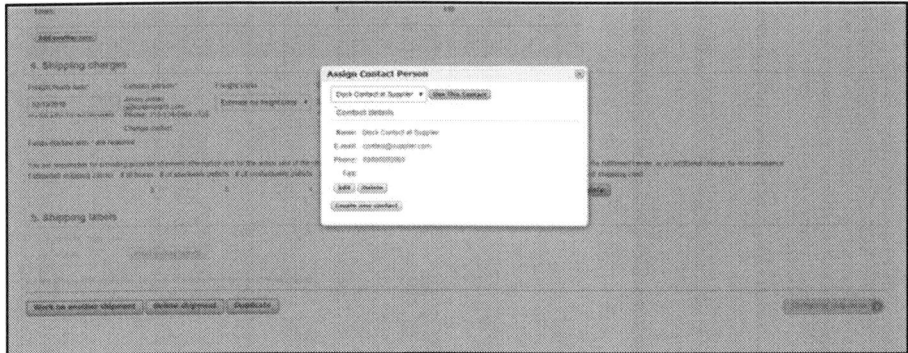

To change the contact information, click on "Change contact". The next screen will allow you to save several contacts for future use.

When the contact information has been confirmed, click "Calculate" to see the charges for the LTL shipment.

Just as with SPD shipments, these charges are deducted from your Amazon seller account, but unlike SPD shipments, you do not have a choice in the carrier selected by Amazon. If you do not agree with the charges, your only option is to cancel the shipment. The carriers who haul shipments for Amazon work in a "Carrier Pool", and similar to a round-robin scenario, carriers are selected in sequence according to variables that are not disclosed to Professional Sellers.

Step 7 – Shipping and Pallet Labels

The shipping labels are now ready to download and/or print. For SPD shipments, there will be one unique label per box. For LTL shipments, there will be a set of four (4) labels for each pallet. Also, for LTL shipments, case labels can also be created.

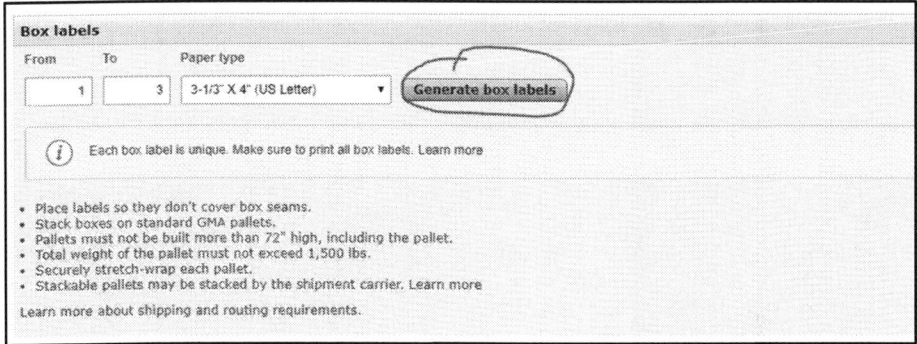

Codes are printed on all labels to provide information about the product, the preparation needed, the store owner's name and inventory levels. If your supplier is sending the shipment directly to Amazon, save the file as a PDF instead of printing it. Send the PDF file to your supplier via email and you are essentially done with the shipment.

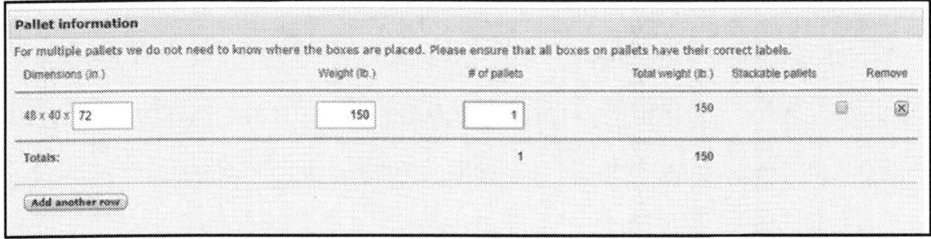

Always insure that there are four (4) pallet labels when preparing a pallet shipment. If you have more than one pallet, click "Add another row" to enter the specifics for the other pallet. The supplier will affix the shipping labels to the cases and/or the shrink wrap around the pallet and ship the pallet(s) to Amazon. Suppliers may charge extra to affix the interior case labels, so it is your choice.

In a few days after the shipment is submitted, Amazon will notify you that the Bill of Lading (BOL) is ready. Just download that file and send it via email to your supplier. Your interaction is not needed for that document, but the supplier needs it to prepare for the LTL carrier's pickup.

Depending on your supplier's fees and your comfort level of ensuring that cases will not be lost at the Amazon warehouse, you may wish to have the supplier apply a case label to each case on the pallet, in addition to the pallet labels on the outside shrink wrap.

When I sent my very first pallet to Amazon, the supplier convinced me that the pallet labels on the shrink wrap were enough and case labels were optional, and not required. The supplier also advised that taking the time to apply case labels to each case on the pallet would cost .25 per case. At time of the order, I had 116 cases on the pallet. The items that I was sending to Amazon were small, and the cases were built in an interlocking pattern to maintain support throughout transport.

I was explained to me that the pallet was already built and that tearing it down to apply case labels would take extra time. The supplier would be willing to do it, but there would be extra effort and costs involved. I got the impression that they would affix the case labels if they HAD to, but they really did not WANT to. The supplier also advised that "no other customer applied the case labels, and nothing has ever gone wrong". I know they were trying to provide reassurance that all would be fine with only the pallet shipment labels, but I had a gut-feeling, an emotional red flag, that was telling me differently. After much deliberation and calculating the extra costs to apply the cases labels, I decided not to label the cases and affix only the four (4) pallet shipping labels to the pallet. In hindsight, the gut-feeling needed to be taken seriously.

Although it is not shown in real-time, you can monitor the check-in by watching the receive count increase in your inventory as the items are scanned in.

I found out several days later that the pallet arrived at the Amazon warehouse intact, but after the employee started "checking in" the cases, the pallet shrink wrap was removed and thrown away. Now, my cases were exposed, not labeled and sitting on a generic pallet on the Receiving Dock. If the employee had continued in the check-in process without interruption, all would be fine; however, in this case, the employee was interrupted or otherwise re-directed away from my pallet. When someone else attempted to check-in the items, there was no labeling to identify the products as mine. The pallet was relocated to an area of the warehouse similar to "lost and found", and the check-in process stopped. Of the 330 items that I shipped via 116 cases on one pallet, only 18 items had been checked in before the employee was pulled away. In this case, I watched in Seller Central as the check-in number stalled and stopped its increase from 18, even after several days. When I created a Seller Support case to inquire on the status, I was advised that there is a window of time allowed for the check-in process to be completed, and I needed to wait 14 business days before an official investigation could be opened. Well, I just knew in my gut that something was wrong. By the time the investigative case could be opened, too much time had passed. The result of the investigation was that the items were declared "lost" and they would not be checked into my store's inventory. To initiate a request for reimbursement, I was required to send in an invoice to show my costs for the missing items. In this case, Amazon took partial responsibility for losing the items and reimbursed me at 90% of my total costs. According to the Seller Support representative, if the cases had the correct shipping labels on them, the items would not have been lost and any employee could have continued the check-in process during the 14-day receiving timeframe. This insight is not provided anywhere – it is a true "learn-by-fire" scenario. Although I received a reimbursement for 90% of my purchase costs, I was still hurt financially because I had to write off the remaining 10% of the costs. Additionally, the shipping charges of transporting the items to Amazon now seemed to be an unnecessary expense. In the end, the biggest hurt was not being able to recognize sales from the items and having to reorder products all over again. A lot of time, energy and money was needlessly spent simply because the shipping labels were not applied to the cases.

I am sure that it is easy to apply judgment in this case and wonder how I could have missed something so "obvious". Being my first shipment, I wanted to watch overall costs. I opted out of applying the case shipping labels because I wanted to save money, and I trusted my supplier's advice. Just because this worked without delays for other customers, does not mean that it would work for me. I had faith in my supplier, but not faith in myself – in my gut feeling. I do not fault the supplier because based on his experience, he never experienced any previous troubles – and why would he? Once the pallet leaves his dock, there is no reason to advise him of progress or delays related to the shipment. I am not living in regret over this situation, but I have certainly learned from it.

When you start your store, one way to avoid getting "hurt" is to request that the supplier affix the shipping labels to the cases on a pallet. Spending a few extra dollars for this service is certainly better than losing items at the warehouse, and ultimately missing out on sales, because there are no labels available to identify stranded items as yours.

IX.

Tracking a Shipment.

For FBA inventory, tracking a shipment of bulk items to an Amazon Fulfillment Center is conducted in Seller Central. Log into the back-office, and under "Inventory", select "Manage FBA Shipments". This area will show the status of all your shipments and the progress of the items being checked into physical inventory. Click on the shipment status you are interested in and the details of the shipping progress will be displayed. Any time after the shipment has been completed, you may review the contents of the shipment by clicking on "Download SKU List" from the View Shipments screen – just like we did when double-checking the contents of the shipping plan. You may download the shipping contents text file. I usually print out the file. Once Amazon notifies me that a shipment has been completely checked-in, I use the printout to reconcile the items shipped versus active items available for sale in my inventory. Any discrepancies, after the allowance of

14 business days for the receiving process, can be identified and reported to Seller Support.

Shipments to customers from Amazon can also be viewed in Seller Central. Log into the back-office and under "Orders", select "Manage Orders". When an order is fulfilled, an automated notification is sent to your email on file to advise that an item has been shipped, but you can review this area of Seller Central for specific order details.

X.

Customer Interaction

Account Health

The biggest benefit of being a "Professional Seller" on the Amazon platform is that all the costs for targeted marketing campaigns, website optimization, lead generation, product promotion, customer service, fulfillment and merchant services are bundled together for one low monthly cost. This structure evens the playing field for all sellers because everyone has the same level of benefits. In exchange for a highly-monetized structure, Professional Sellers are bound to high standards. These standards are in place to protect Amazon's reputation, product quality and selection, and control of market saturation, but most of all, this structure increases customer retention. Amazon's consistent growth shows that customers trust the stability of Amazon. To deliver on their priority mission of providing the best customer experience, and to maintain that relationship, Professional Sellers have a responsibility to act responsibly.

"Seller Central" is the back-office where the entire picture of your online store's activity is monitored. One feature is called "Account Health", a visual picture of the potential perception of your online store in the eyes of the marketplace – the consumer. Communication with and ratings from buyers is crucial to good Account Health. If your online store's Account Health is poor, Amazon may decide to shut down your store – forever! Stores closed for poor Account Health are not reopened. Before this decision is made, however, Amazon is fair, and they contact you with suggestions on how to improve your Account Health. If you do not respond, or the Account Health does not improve within a provided amount of time, your online store could be shut down.

Having good Account Health is not only good for Amazon and the customer, but it is also good for your relationships with your suppliers. Wholesalers, distributors, manufacturers and resellers who are familiar with Amazon tend to review your online store's customer ratings and reviews. If they are low, they may decide to decline your request for service, decline long-pay terms, or they may charge you higher rates than they charge other sellers who have better ratings.

To check your Account Health Dashboard, log into your Seller Central, and the "Performance" tab, click "Account Health".

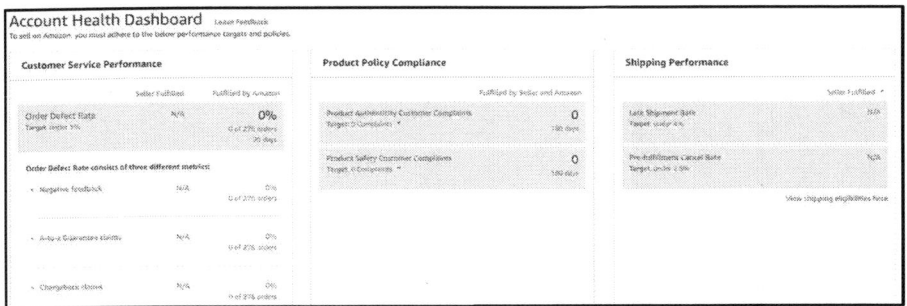

On the dashboard, you can quickly review your status against their defined metrics. Adhering to these metrics ensures that you will be able to continue selling on the Amazon platform. Any metrics that fall short of its goal should be addressed immediately. While there are several metrics available for review, the "Performance Metrics" are a key indicator to your overall account health. The "Performance Metrics" can be viewed by both the items "Seller Fulfilled" and "Fulfilled by Amazon" categories. As long as the status is Green, your account health is good. Any other status should be addressed immediately.

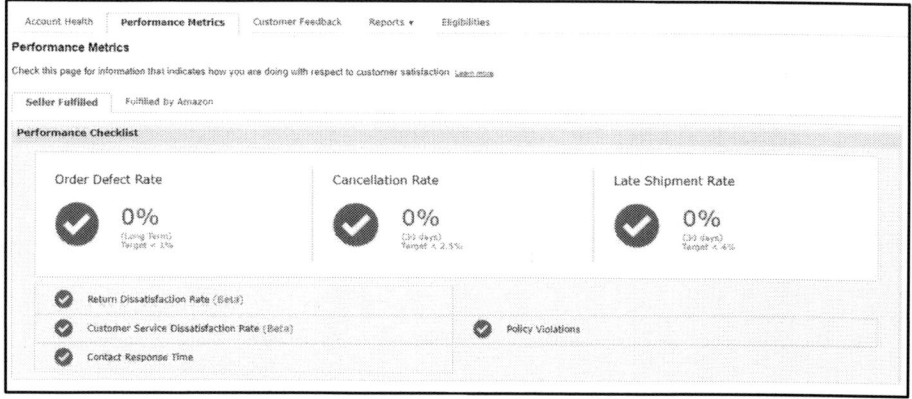

A partnership with Amazon and their carriers provides faster service to the customer and overall better rating for your online store. The better the rating, the more your potential listings will appear when a customer conducts a search for your product. For Amazon, their highest mission is to provide the best customer experience. The sooner you align with that mindset, the better your online store will operate.

Stars and Reviews, while used by many online platforms to rate a consumer's experience with a product and service, Amazon uses this information to determine the rank of a product in a category, and the overall account health of a seller's store.

If reviews are low or non-existent, the store's health is rated low. Of course, when you are just starting out, Amazon knows it will take time to build up organic reviews. Organic reviews are highly preferred as they come from actual purchasers of your products. There are some sellers who try to generate false reviews in an attempt to improve store health. Amazon has an algorithm to determine which reviews are real and which are contrived. I suggest that you focus on operating your store with integrity with real reviews and do not waste time with trying to "fool the system".

When you start your store, one way to avoid getting "hurt" is to avoid spending valuable time trying to fabricate reviews for products in your inventory. It is better to allow the reviews to flow in organically.

Buyer Messages

Buyer messages play a large role in determining the health of your account. These messages are usually from potential buyers interested in buying a product, but they have a question about the product's size, features or ability to function in a certain way, and, believe it or not, the responsiveness to their question – not so much the answer – will determine if they buy from you or your competitor.

Amazon requires that you respond to a buyer's message within 24 hours – seven days a week – in order to maintain good Account Health. When I first heard this, my thought was that I would be bound to the inbox every day all day long hoping not to miss a message. I created calendar reminders to check for messages every 12 hours, and set up notifications to alert me via email if a message arrived. I felt that I would be chained to a business that I believed was going to give me freedom and financial stability.

When you work directly with a supplier and the product is sent directly to an Amazon fulfillment center, it is hard to answer questions without having directly seen or used the product. I believe Amazon wants us to be on-guard, standing at the ready, to answer these questions quickly. I soon figured out the real requirement, and developed a work around that satisfied the standard, and brought me relief.

The requirement from Amazon is that all messages must be responded to within 24 hours. I first misread this to think that I had to provide the answer or an actual solution to the question. My head was spinning wondering how I would find answers from my supplier after hours or on weekends. But then, I realized that I could respond with a polite message that thanked the buyer for the message, and advised that someone would respond with an answer as soon as possible. The response could be saved as a template in Notepad, and pasted as soon as the message arrived. While this didn't answer their question, it met Amazon's requirement to respond. This strategy only bought me a little bit of time because I did not want the customer to buy from someone else; however, having it reduce my stress was very welcomed.

Returns and Customer Service

Among the many benefits of being a Professional Seller, the management of Product Returns and Customer Service are so invaluable. I can only imagine the hassles associated with tracking and receiving back returned products. Amazon recently changed the protocol regarding product returns to improve the customer experience. In the past, when a customer received an item that eventually turned out to be undesirable, or was received damaged, the customer would call in, receive an authorization to return the item, Amazon would credit the customer's account, and mark the item as damaged in the seller's active inventory in the back-office. Amazon would then notify the seller to submit a "Removal Order" that would remove the damaged item from storage and ship it back to the seller. Alternatively, Amazon could destroy the item.

The new policy is to acknowledge the customer's desire to return an item, credit the customer's account, mark the item as damaged in the seller's active inventory in the back-office, but now the customer keeps the item. The customer does not have to return ship any products. This is good because, if the product truly is damaged or defective, there is no need to pay for a "Removal Order". This is bad because customers with improper motives can report that a truly suitable product is damaged or defective, and Amazon has no evidence to prove otherwise. The customer's account is simply credited. This diminishes the quantity of suitable inventory and is, in essence, a business loss.

While the request to return product is certainly a large portion of customer service inquiries at the call center, there are a number of other types of calls managed by Amazon, such as shipping durations, product questions, availability of inventory, discussion of price, promotions and much more. Providing staff to respond to these calls is included in the monthly service fee charged to Professional Seller. Honestly, because I do not have to answer the questions day in and day out, I feel relief and the freedom to move about my environment knowing that my customers are receiving the absolute best experience.

Ratings and Asking for Feedback

When an order has been fulfilled, the customer experience cycle is not yet completed. To understand how to get more products in front of a potential buyer, it is important to understand how Amazon scores each online store. As discussed earlier, stars for an online store are important.

To improve the star-rating of your online store within Amazon, customers will rate your products and the overall experience by assigning "stars" to the order.

Amazon provides a limited amount of customer data in Seller Central, but it is enough to send a request to a customer asking for feedback and a star-rating. The customer is sent an email asking them to complete a review of the product and their overall customer experience. The more stars assigned, the better the experience. Prime® online stores with higher average stars, with the lowest price, are shown first after a customer searches for a product to buy.

Stores with fewer stars experience listings further down the list of available products, even if the price is lower. Of course,

Amazon uses an algorithm to determine which products appear in the search yield, and all we can do is maintain every area possible with integrity.

XI.

Payments and Deposits

During the verification process of establishing your Professional Seller account, Amazon validates your business checking account so that payments due to you can be directly deposited on regular intervals. Additionally, the account will be debited for the monthly account fee, any transit and prep fees, or chargebacks for products returned by the customer. Amazon will keep a balance on record in your back-office until the automatic payment period arrives, or until you request a transfer to your bank account. There is a possibility that the amount automatically transferred will be less than the balance on record because Amazon holds back a "reserve" amount based on the number of products that could potentially be returned. They have sophisticated algorithms that determine the reserve amount, and the Seller Support representatives cannot change this reserve amount. Eventually, the reserve is released into your bank account. This action is very similar to when a hotel places an authorization on your credit card in anticipation of ancillary charges during your overnight stay. Once you check out of the room, with no damages or extra charges, the authorization expires. Amazon holds back a reserve amount in anticipation of any possible fees that could be charged to your seller account. Once it determines that there are no forecasted or potential extra charges, it will release the funds. It is important to have other financial resources available to purchase products from your selected suppliers so that you do not rely on the balance in the checking account to conduct business. I found it a best practice to have and use a company credit card – a business credit card opened under my company name – for ordering products from suppliers, while using the seller account funds for Amazon back-office transactions. You may want to have a setup that operates differently, and that is acceptable. It is your store, so do what is right for you – within the Amazon guidelines.

XII.

Legal, Taxes and Reports in Amazon

Seller Central offers a host of reports to track inventory, shipping, sales and taxes. As each business has different goals and requirements, it is best to review the available reports to analyze your specific company's performance. Log into Seller Central and click on the "Reports" tab to see the various reports available. Some reports can be viewed on screen, and others can only be downloaded. Additionally, some reports can compile data for only a single 30-day period at a time, while others can capture the entire year of activity. It is best to jump in and see which reports are most useful for you. At the time of this writing, Amazon may soon implement the ability to customize some of the reports.

To determine if your online store is meeting all the requirements of laws or taxes in your state, contact a professional who can guide you accordingly.

XIII.

Support and Troubleshooting

Most every aspect of Amazon is automated – access to Seller Support Representatives is limited and finding the contact number to the Seller Support Center is not easy. Amazon publishes a series of help blogs to answer common questions, and the information is very high-level. Sending an email to the Seller Support Center will open an automated case that creates auto-responders to communicate information and status. An actual representative will respond within approximately 24-48 hours depending on the nature of your request and the time the email was sent. I found that starting a new case after midnight generates an immediate template response – just a form letter inserted into a reply message from a rep. In my opinion, these responses are frustrating and annoying. I believe that their only purpose is to keep the "Time to Respond" metric low – they rarely provide any real assistance. Sometimes after midnight, I have found myself in a back-and-forth "battle" with a representative who continues to respond with template answers.

To avoid frustration, start the Seller Support Case during regular working hours. It may take a little longer for the answer to be provided, but the response will be thoughtful and pertinent to your question. I do not know if Amazon is aware of this discrepancy, or if it is purposely designed to be this way. Regardless, this work-around has helped reduce my frustration.

XIV.

Conclusion: Now what?

Congratulations on taking your first step to success. As mentioned earlier, Amazon's platform has generated many successful entrepreneurs and created financial freedom for many people around the world. This book does not cover everything you will eventually learn along the way to success, but it is the first step. There is still much to learn about advanced selling strategies and techniques as you progress. Analyze each strategy, technique or tool to see if it is a fit for you. Do what you feel is right for your preferred level of involvement, desired income and product offerings. Utilizing the information, tools and resources in this book is the first step – but it is a step only you can take. Make that step today! Follow the guide presented here, and if you believe you can – then, you can!

Want more?

Through direct hands-on experience, and with feedback gained by coaching others in their online store set-up, I have learned that having someone beside you through the setup of your online store is invaluable to your success. The journey has been previously travelled and learning with someone who has already trudged the path can help you immensely. Phone conferences can be arranged to fit your schedule and budget. To discuss your specific needs, visit my website at www.StartAmazonStore.com and drop me a line to let me know what you need. I will respond with ideas and suggestions customized for you. Also, once you've implemented the steps to start your store, I would love to hear about your successes.

XV.

Directory of Resources

Business Entity – www.nolo.com

EIN – Employer Identification Number – https://www.irs.gov/businesses/small-businesses-self-employed/apply-for-an-employer-identification-number-ein-online

DUNS Number – Dun and Bradstreet Business Credit Profile - https://www.sba.gov/contracting/getting-started-contractor/get-d-u-n-s-number

Texas Resale Certificate – also known as a Tax-exempt Certificate – https://comptroller.texas.gov/taxes/sales/forms/

XVI.

Testimonials

What Others are Saying...

Lori Dunham is all about business. Her exceptional work fires her enthusiasm and defines her focus. Her ability to consider introspective aspects allows difficult life lessons to be reframed for the creation of launching pads. She is bold enough for toe-to-toe negotiations with the high*est* ups, and she is willing to stay the course when challenges arise. One strength that most impresses me is Lori's ability to initiate difficult conversations and to see them through with confidence and compassion. Like the aviator narrator in Saint-Exupery's *The Little Prince*, Lori is one of the rare "grown-ups" who will say *Yes!* to playful adventures and an equally enthusiastic *Yes!* to complicated, focused agendas.

- **LL Parker**

"Lori's exceptional work fires her enthusiasm and defines her focus. She handles tough negotiations and she stays the course when challenges arise. She executes every task diligently and in a way that only she can. She is a superb leader!"

- **Adriana Franco**

Lori falls asleep with a dream and wakes up with a purpose! Everything she achieves is done with precision, motivation and determination. She is the pure definition of unstoppable. She doesn't wait for opportunities to arise, she creates them!

- **Mandy Pember**
Mandy's Studio, Arlington, TX
www.facebook.com/mandysstudio11

I am very excited to congratulate Lori on her first book! The day that I learned of this accomplishment made me very proud of her. Within the last six years, I have seen her grow leaps and bounds. She has inspired me and others to understand that with a positive attitude and continuous hard work, without ever losing hope, we can reach greater heights. I have seen her accept people with love, always being full of laughter and always having a smile on her face. My hope for her is to go far in this life and help many people along the way. Here's to many more books from her!

— **Roshni Dhatingan**

About the Author

Lori Dunham is a business owner, public speaker, mentor and author. Her mission is to inspire and encourage others to take their first step toward their dream. In many cases, the first step is the hardest step to take, especially without support. It is her desire that this book helps others find the courage and resources necessary to take action, live their dreams, and leave a legacy to be proud of!

Made in the USA
Columbia, SC
23 March 2018